A Woman's World

A
Woman's World

A Christian Psychologist Discusses
Twelve Common Problem Areas

by

CLYDE M. NARRAMORE, Ed. D.

ZONDERVAN PUBLISHING HOUSE
GRAND RAPIDS   MICHIGAN

A WOMAN'S WORLD
Copyright 1963 by
Zondervan Publishing House
Grand Rapids, Michigan

Library of Congress Catalog Card No. 63 - 15733

Second Printing — September, 1963

1242685

LIST OF CHAPTERS

1. When a Woman Is at Her Best.................. 9

2. Your Emotional and Mental Well-Being.......... 23

3. The Woman Outside the Home.................. 53

4. The Unmarried Woman........................ 65

5. The Immature Husband....................... 86

6. Married to an Unbeliever......................101

7. The Dilemma of Young Mothers................114

8. When Love Is Not There......................129

9. The Maladjusted Child........................149

10. Extra Family Members........................167

11. Sex Problems in Marriage.....................181

12. Growing Spiritually 197

ACKNOWLEDGMENTS

A Woman's World is filled with interesting people, some radiant and happy, others heavily laden with problems. Although these illustrations are about real people, information has been altered so that no one can be identified. Names throughout the book have been arbitrarily assigned and have no resemblance to any person whatsoever, living or dead. Most illustrations are composite, bearing the characteristics of several people who have had similar experiences.

Special recognition is given to those who have had part in the planning, development, typing, editing and reviewing of the manuscript: Gloria Bowen, Eleanor Cory, Forrest Forbes, Alice Elliott, Richard T. Laird, Mary McKinney, Ruth Narramore, Donald Robertson, Millard Sall and Benjamin Weiss.

Grateful appreciation is also expressed to the many fine Christian women who have placed their confidence in the author and who have helped to make his work possible.

A Woman's World

CHAPTER ONE

When a Woman Is at Her Best

For the past hour the hands of the clock seemed to race around in half the time. It was nearly noon and Louise was deftly putting last-minute touches on the table. Barbara, a former chum, was coming for lunch and the afternoon. It had been years since they had seen each other.

I wonder whether she's changed much, mused Louise. *She was always so attractive and clever.* A score of happy experiences were running through her mind when the doorbell suddenly interrupted. Louise stole a last appraising glance in the hall mirror and quickly adjusted a stubborn lock of hair. Then she swung open the door and there stood Barbara — a little older, naturally, but as pretty and as pert as ever.

The two embraced, exchanged greetings and laughed a little. Then, after a delightful luncheon, they settled down for a good, satisfying time of chatting and reminiscing.

Later that evening Louise sank down in an easy chair and began to thumb through a magazine. But her eyes didn't seem to reach the page. She kept thinking of Barbara's accomplishments and, even more, of the years which she, herself, had sandwiched in since she had graduated from school.

The thoughts and pictures that unfolded in her mind brought a mixture of feelings — some warm with satisfaction, some almost bordering on the giddy, others with regret, and still others with a tinge of uncertainty. But these experiences, significant as they were, could not compare in importance with those which, in the years to come, would stretch out before Louise.

She could not change, nor even rearrange, the years that were now behind her. Those pages were already written. But the days and years ahead were still untouched, waiting for the choices she would make to determine her world.

Every one of us lives in a world of our own. You may be happy in it, or you may wish situations were different. Yet, no matter how you view your world, like Louise, your future depends largely on you. This does not imply that you are the master of your own destiny, or the captain of your own fate. The poet who held to this shaky creed did not reckon with God, the Captain of our souls. Indeed, God is over all and has the whole world in His hands. But this does not relieve us of personal responsibility. Everyone has been endowed with some talent or ability. With God's help your life can spell progression, and not regression, as the years go on. Wise choices will lead to fulfillment, not disillusionment. The future is yours to mold, and it does not necessarily have to follow the patterns of the past.

Womanhood

You have a special place to fill by just being a woman. When God created a companion for the first man in the Garden of Eden, He endowed her with the attributes of beauty, gentleness, love, a sensitive nature and an understanding heart. These have become the symbols of womanhood. They form the framework for development for every little girl as she grows and matures and then blossoms into a lovely young lady.

You are the inspiration, the world over, for story, song, poem, and painting. You are the symbol of hospitality and service. You were last at the cross, first at the tomb, first to tell of the resurrection, first to proclaim redemption to the Jews, first to greet Christian missionaries, and the first European convert. You contributed to the comfort of our Lord, you washed the Saviour's feet and anointed His head with ointment. You were the mother of Christ, our Lord.

You hold a place of honor. You are the image of queenliness and the essence of virtue. Because of this, you have won men's respect.

God thought so highly of woman that He placed the One dearest to His heart in her arms as a tiny babe, to be loved and cared for. What greater honor could there be — the mother of the Son of God!

The greatest trust in all the world is in the hands of a woman. It becomes her responsibility to mold and to shape human lives in her role of motherhood. Her influence has no limit. A godly mother may mark the pathway for generations to follow, and in this way sway the destinies of the world.

Are you a mother? Then you know the joys and trials that confront you day by day. But do you see the challenge? Down through the centuries mothers have been the key to the success or failure of their offspring. More than a century ago, a frontier mother left her mark upon an awkward country boy. The gaunt and lonely Lincoln standing as a rock in a broken land could say of her: "All that I am, or ever hope to be, I owe to my angel mother."

A busy woman in England was responsible for helping to shape the spiritual history of two continents. Susanna Wesley was the mother of nineteen children, two of whom were the renowned John and Charles Wesley. In such a large brood it is said that the children were permitted the luxury of crying, but only in a quiet voice and in proper turn. Yet they knew the impress of their mother, Susanna, who prayed with each one alone every day. They were led to Christ as young men and their ministry was one of fruitful blessing. The memory of their lives and of their outstanding Christian leadership is a fitting tribute to their godly mother.

Whether you are married or single, whether you are a mother or have never had any children of your own, your life as a woman is one of influence. The poet aptly penned this thought in the following lines:

*They talk about a woman's sphere as though it had a
    limit;
There's not a place in earth or Heaven,
There's not a task to mankind given,
There's not a blessing or a woe,*

There's not a whispered yes or no,
There's not a life, or death, or birth,
That has a feather's weight of worth—without a woman
       in it.   C. E. Bowman

As a woman you are an interesting combination of the
idealistic and the practical. Your sensitive nature and noble
heart encourage idealism, while the very nature of your
responsibilities demand that you accept the practical. A
proper balance between the two is desirable and necessary.
A woman with a great aspiration but no roots may find
herself bankrupt and disillusioned. On the other hand, to
succumb to the drab routine of practical everyday living
can rob a woman of her sparkle and charm. Diapers and
dishes, dishes and diapers — day in, day out — the monotony
of humdrum activities takes its toll. This woman is tired and
bored. She is in a rut where her only diversion is self-pity.
How easy it is for such a woman to just settle down in the
status quo! And how deadly to her personality and self-
development.

Design for Growing

As a woman you owe it to yourself and to others to
"be somebody" to someone. You must keep moving if you
do not want to become stagnant. You must have a source to
draw from and an outlet for expression. You cannot stand
still. You must grow — or shrivel. The law of the universe
demands it.

Personal growth is a continual process. One never
graduates from the school of life. There is always more to
learn, and the more we learn, the more enriched our lives
become, and the more interesting we are to those about us.

Any observing person knows that a woman's life is
crammed with petty details. These often usurp her time and
prevent her from doing many of the things that she would
otherwise enjoy. She seems destined to detail — there's a
stitch to be sewed, a cake to be baked, a dress to be pressed.
As a mother, she must nurse a wounded knee, prod a poky
piano practicer, or serve as referee when young wills clash.
Small things to be sure — but so time consuming. These daily

duties *are* demanding, yet they need not deter your personal growth. Nothing can keep you from personal development without your permission. If you are not satisfied to remain static, if you are unwilling to bury your God-given talents, then, where there's a will there's a way. Growth does not necessarily need to take place under ideal conditions. You may live in uninspiring circumstances, or be surrounded by somewhat uninteresting people, yet you can be the exception to the rule. Stately pines often grow on a rocky ledge. If you wait for the "perfect time," it will never come. Growth is a result of attitude. Determine that you will not be the same tomorrow as you are today, then pray and persist in your purpose.

Growth seldom happens in a dramatic way, dramatic as it may be when you look back. It is a way of life, a day-by-day experience growing out of dedication to a purpose. Women such as Clara Barton, Florence Nightingale, Carrie Jacobs Bond, Marie Curie, Evangeline Booth, Frances Siewert and multitudes of others have carried the banner of purpose and have won. You may not reach the public pinnacle they have; but you can be a blessing and an inspiration to your children and your friends. You will be happier and more satisfied because you have enriched your environment and developed your potential. But most of all, you will have fulfilled God's plan for your life. He wants His *best* for you.

Mental Stimulation

Thumb back through the pages of your experience and re-read a chapter in your childhood. You are in elementary school. The teacher throws out a question and immediately several hands shoot up. It's the same ones who consistently wave their hands in response to teacher's questions. These are the "smart kids," and, interestingly enough, mostly girls. The boys, because of their later development, will have their opportunity to shine later on.

What happens to all those "smart little girls" when they grow up? Not many of them will become doctors or lawyers like their male counterparts. Some will become teachers or office workers. But the majority of these bright girls will grow up to be mothers and homemakers. Many of them will become leaders in the community. They have keen minds that demand a challenge; without it, they become the victims of frustration and boredom.

You are an intelligent being. God has given you an inquiring mind. Yet, unless you are satisfying its demand for mental stimulation, you will become stale and uninteresting.

Intelligence is not a quality chiefly cornered by the male sex or by a few gifted women. Every person has intellectual qualities. Unfortunately, some women become so involved in the daily routine of the home or office that they squelch their intellectuality. The important factor is not merely what you learn, but also your own attitude toward self-development. When you see the value of continued growth, the circumstances around you can become stepping stones. Much of the knowledge you assimilate in life is gained in an informal manner. When you learn to sharpen your powers of discernment and train yourself to be more observant, a whole new world will unfold before you. Even the commonplace will take on new meaning.

The alert woman recognizes opportunities for mental stimulation in many forms. Even helping your youngster with his school work can be a real source of learning to *you*. Times have changed since you were in the classroom. With the increased knowledge of our scientific society, textbooks are outdated in just a few years. So your children are learning many things that were not even known until recently. Although you won't be filling a classroom seat, you do have the opportunity to learn as you help your children.

Don't wait for your husband to give you the signal to grow. You may even have to lead the way. He may not realize how intellectually stifling your situation is for you. He may be in a job where he must read and talk with others, or where he has the opportunity of taking business trips and meeting interesting people. Be that as it may, you have a responsibility to yourself, as well as to your husband. So while he is growing in his experiences, take the initiative to grow in your own right.

Intellectual growth is rewarding for its own sake, but it also has its by-products. You gain in confidence and self-respect, the world becomes a more fascinating place, and you become a more interesting person.

The Reading Habit

Today, interesting books are piled high almost everywhere you look. Yet, despite this open road to the printed page, many people spend little time reading. This is especially true of women.

"I don't have time," said one homemaker. "My days are so full with caring for the children, doing home chores, committee meetings, taking the older children to and from various activities, and a multitude of other things, that I don't have a free moment to myself. After dinner there's dishes, getting the younger ones into bed, and taking care of a dozen other jobs. By the time everything quiets down I'm so weary I can't concentrate. So I just turn on the TV for a little relaxation before I go to bed."

It is obvious why *that* woman does not do more reading. And there are many others like her. Even magazines are often not much more than skimmed through.

Busy women, however, need not give up the joys and the benefits of reading. If need be, cut something else out of your crowded schedule and give at least a little time for Christian books and magazines. Even if you assimilate it bite size, it will give you mental and spiritual nourishment. It is essential to your personal growth, and your family should not be permitted to rob you of this necessity. If they do, they will suffer too.

Your world may be a limited one, but you can push back the horizons by developing the habit of reading. As you pick up a book you can make the acquaintance of the greatest people of all time. Circumstances may prevent you from ever meeting such people in person. Your contacts may be limited to those in your immediate locality. Not so with reading. Here you have a passport to explore a world of interesting, creative personalities. The ideas gathered from the printed page will become some of the strongest forces in your life.

The fact that reading can be so flexible is a boon to the average busy woman. Unlike walking away from someone in person, you can leave a book whenever you wish. Any time you come back, its pages will still be waiting for you, pleasant as before.

Joan was a secretary in a large law firm. She was also a wife and homemaker, so her time was well occupied. However, she knew the value of reading and always tried to keep a fine Christian book in her desk at the office. During coffee breaks and rest periods she pulled out her "friend in print" and read a little. It was only a matter of time before she reached the final chapter, and then it was time to begin another book. The result was that Joan was well informed. And the payoff came when her boss decided that a girl of her calibre should be promoted to a more responsible position.

"That's all right for the business girl," you may say, "but how about those of us who spend our time being nursemaid, housekeeper, and chief cook and bottle-washer for an active, growing family? Where do we find time to read?"

It may be impossible for you to devote a solid block of time to reading, but to "sandwich it in between" may give you just the lift you need. Marilyn proved that it can be done. With several small children around and under foot, she had little time for anything other than the "three C's": *caring, cleaning, and cooking.* But she found that by squeezing in a few minutes here and there, she could read a short article, or a few pages, at one sitting without upsetting her time schedule. This enabled her to "get out of the house" for awhile, as it were, to meet new, interesting people, and to tickle her imagination with new ideas. For Marilyn, these "reading breaks" were a form of rejuvenation which made it easier to accomplish the many tasks that were hers each day.

The printed page is a powerful force. Probably more information takes root in your mind by this means than by any other medium. Unfortunately, Satan is aware of this and herein lies a pitfall. Reading, like many other activities which are beneficial, can also be detrimental. Satan has poisoned a goodly share of printed material. It is better not to read at all than to feed on the devil's trash. However, there are countless volumes of unusual value. And for all the *trash*, there is just as much *treasure*.

Since reading provides intellectual food, it is essential that spiritual nourishment be a sizable part of your diet. Indeed, Christian books and magazines should comprise the bulk of your reading. It is in this way that you gain spiritual insight and grow in the Lord.

Dotty, for example, fed her mind on trash. She read dime novels by the dozen. *Real Confessions, True Love, Night Life* — these and other magazines like them had become her steady diet. But she hadn't read a Christian book in years. In time, Dotty became just like her reading material — cheap and ordinary. Although there are many who scorn the cheap literature of Dotty's choice, still *they never read anything that feeds the soul or draws them closer to Christ.* Such women may accumulate a store of information and secular knowledge, but they are ignorant of godly wisdom. Their Christian growth is stunted and, as a result, they remain spiritually immature.

Today's Christian bookstores are bulging with attractive books that are longing to be read. Biographies, novels, devotional books and many other volumes vie for your attention. To have such Christ-honoring literature within your grasp is an opportunity and a privilege. Thomas Jefferson once said, "I cannot live without books." Indeed, you and I can say, "I cannot live *well* without them."

Your Aesthetic Qualities

Personal growth would be incomplete without the fineness of aesthetic appreciation. This is a quality that makes you more human and, at the same time, more noble. To neglect the aesthetic side of your nature is to take color out of your sight. Aesthetic experiences provide emotional release. They deepen your sensitivity and awaken the best in you. The Bible admonishes, ". . . whatsoever things are pure, whatsoever things are lovely . . . think on these things" (Philippians 4:8).

Unfortunately, some women have become so closely bound by their seven-day work-week rut that they rarely take time to develop this area of their lives. Yet, a woman's personality demands cultural development. Your complex, sensitive nature remains most feminine as you have aesthetic experiences.

Your grandmother likely lived in a simple environment where the aesthetic treasures of nature were at her fingertips. She arose with the surge of a fiery sun breaking through the gray dawn in the glorious victory of a sunrise. In the garden and field she watched things grow. Then as day drew to a close she was often engulfed in a blaze of dramatic glory while the sinking sun flung a spectrum of brilliance across the western sky. These experiences surrounded her daily. They were a part of her life. The extent of her aesthetic enjoyment depended, however, upon the depth of her appreciation. Even in the midst of beauty there are some who are not moved.

Today's woman lives in a different kind of world. She is likely to be existing on a sparse diet of cement streets, blaring horns, raucous radios, noisy television, soaring skyscrapers and other artificial surroundings. However, even amid a setting so uninspiring as this, beauty is waiting for those who are willing to see and listen. It may be found in a song, in a sunbeam, or in a smile. It is there for those who would find it, making life richer and fuller because it was not overlooked.

The greater your understanding and experience, the deeper will be your appreciation. The gifted musician, with years of musical background, has a greater capacity to enjoy the tonal intricacies of a symphony than does the average untrained ear. The artist has a keener sense of color value and composition than does the average bystander. Thus, by increasing your knowledge of the arts, you broaden the scope of your aesthetic experiences.

Modern civilization is often derided because of its artificial environment. Nevertheless, it does provide certain cultural advantages. Do you avail yourself of them? When was the last time you visited a museum, allowing your mind to exercise itself in facts interwoven with fancy? Do you ever free yourself to attend a concert, or hear a special lecture? Perhaps you live in an area of natural beauty. Yet, tourists may have seen more of these natural wonders than you.

There is solid truth in the old proverb, "The best things in life are free." God has provided the matchless beauties of the universe, and they are yours to enjoy. It is an aesthetically depraved soul who is not moved at the grandeur of the mighty Rockies or awed with wonder at the intricate magnificence of a rose. The thundering breakers of the ocean must never become commonplace. Golden fields of graceful grain bowing to the rhythm of the breeze must not slip by you unnoticed. You are the loser if you fail to observe the moonlight caressing the desert, or the song of a single thrush. Truly, "The heavens declare the glory of God: and the firmament sheweth His handywork" (Psalm 19:1). We remain poor if we do not fill our souls with the beauty that surrounds us.

Never Too Late

It is never too late to learn. And whether your school days are many years behind you or just a few, it is always time to improve. Then, as you grow personally and develop your abilities, you will gain a sense of satisfaction because you have accomplished something of lasting value.

There are many intelligent women whose lives are out of character with their ability because they lack education and training. This was so in Vivian's case, but she did something about it.

When Vivian graduated from high school she did not go on to college, partly because she lacked finances, but mostly because neither she nor her parents recognized the value of higher education. Vivian took an office job and two years later married Ken, a pre-med student at the university. Her job was a financial necessity during the years of Ken's schooling, but at last those days were over and Ken was a full-fledged doctor.

As the years sped on the couple was blessed with three

lovely children. "What an ideal family!" people said. Yes, they were a happy family, except for one thing. Vivian was frustrated by her lack of education. Ken's associates were professional men with degrees, and most of their wives were college graduates. The fact that she had not gone beyond high school was a "sore spot" in Vivian's self-confidence.

The years continued and the children grew. Now they were all in college. Vivian was intrigued by the courses they were taking and followed their progress with fervent interest. Then she made her decision: *she would go to college, too.* She did, and enjoyed every minute of it. When graduation rolled around, "Mom" and her "baby" (the youngest in the family) received their sheepskins together— with high honors. "We are so proud of Mom," her children told their friends.

Vivian had fulfilled her dream, but little did she realize how valuable that fulfillment was to become. Within a year her husband was stricken with a serious illness and was forced to give up his practice. Because she had the college qualifications, she was able to get a teaching job in the local school. "I always wanted to be a teacher," said Vivian. The school was close, her hours were satisfactory, and the pay was good. But even more, she was doing the kind of work she thoroughly enjoyed.

Many women do not share Vivian's desire to obtain a college education. Indeed, you may have little or no need for a degree. However, you may find it challenging to enroll in special adult classes, taking whatever courses may interest you. It is possible that you may uncover hidden talents. Cynthia's experience bears this out!

Cynthia's life was far from colorful. She and her husband had lived in the same house with the same furniture for more than twenty years. Her husband, a machinist, worked the evening shift, and their nineteen-year-old son was serving his time in the Army, so she was alone a great deal. Cynthia wasn't exactly bored, but neither was she challenged.

One day she picked up a folder which described the adult extension courses offered in the local Junior College.

As she looked it over, an idea flashed across her mind, *Why don't I enroll?* And that's just what she did. She decided to take a practical course — typing. But as she studied the catalog, her eyes seemed to glue themselves on another course, a "non-essential" one. *Oil painting*, she mused. *That's what I've always wanted to do — paint. I wonder — oh, that's probably foolish. I paint? No one in our family ever did anything like that. And yet — I really would like to try my hand at it.*

When Cynthia signed for the typing course she mustered up enough nerve to ask about the course in oil painting.

"Certainly," said the teacher. "You may discover that you have real talent. And if not, who cares? You'll still have the fun of painting." Then, with a smile, the teacher added, "Your 'soul' needs to grow, you know!"

That was all Cynthia needed. Two weeks later she found herself not only in the typing class, but also in the studio, with palette, brush and oils. From then on it was surprisingly easy — and worlds of fun. But that isn't the end of the story. She made a "C" in typing but an "A" in Art. Within a year the secret had gotten out — at church, around the neighborhood, and even to relatives: "Cynthia is becoming an artist — she does oil paintings!"

Indeed, she had not only completed a number of pictures for herself, but she had painted several landscapes for her friends as well.

Her productions weren't all Rembrandts, but they *were* good. Yet, what was happening on the canvas was not nearly so important as what was happening to Cynthia. She had nurtured a new skill, found a new outlet of expression and had developed a new outlook. Life had taken on new zest and she was blossoming forth into a new person.

The story of Cynthia's accomplishments would be a happy one if it ended right there. However, the sequel even surpasses the satisfaction of Cynthia's first experience in growth.

Encouraged by the discovery of her newly found talent

and stimulated by her success, Cynthia decided to enroll in another course the following year. This time it was "Interior Decorating." She was thrilled with what she learned, and before long she incorporated many of the decorating principles in her home. The transformation which took place was rewarding in itself, but when Cynthia's son arrived home from the Army, he was thrilled beyond measure. "Mom," he exclaimed, "I never knew you had it in you!"

The truth of the matter was, neither did Cynthia.

Not all women are free to do what Cynthia did. Some have responsibilities which make it difficult to attend classes or be away from the home. Today, however, there are many fine correspondence courses offered in almost every subject.° In many larger cities a number of excellent educational courses are presented on TV.

Are there talents you have never developed? Even if you were "cheated out" of piano lessons when you were a youngster, you can begin now. You may never develop into a Paderewski, but your life will be richer and more satisfying because you have not neglected the gift that is in you (I Timothy 4:14). So, whether it be music, art, creative writing or any other area of special interest, don't let your dreams die. You may look with admiration (perhaps almost envy) upon women who are exercising their abilities, *but what are you doing about your own God-given gifts?* You miss too much if you are just sitting on the sidelines, and others are deprived of the blessing you could be to them.

Getting started is the key to activity. So, once you clear the first hurdle and bring yourself to sign up for that course, or make arrangements for those lessons, you are well on your way. Before you know it, you will look back with personal satisfaction at the progress *you* have made.°

It is a wise woman who steps through the doors of opportunity and avails herself of training. Such a woman will never grow stale. She becomes a challenge to herself and an inspiration to others.

°For a list of institutions offering biblical and secular correspondence courses, write the author, Box 206, Pasadena, California.

CHAPTER TWO

Your Emotional and Mental Well-Being

"Good emotional and mental health may be defined as a dynamic balance amid the stresses and strains of life."

This was a brief, clear definition which a psychology professor threw out to our graduate class one day at Columbia University. I liked it because it was meaningful and to the point.

Close on the heels of this definition came longer, more complex, fuzzy ones. In fact, it seemed that much of our time during the first few weeks in the class was spent scrutinizing various definitions heralded by noted authors. I can't remember much being said about the *symptoms* and *causes* or even the large numbers of people who were suffering from severe personality problems. But we did tickle our expanding minds with definitions!

Today, having worked in the field for years, and now directing a clinic° where we offer more than one thousand hours of professional counseling each month, I have seen new meanings in emotional and mental problems.

I've learned, for example, that no one is emotionally healthy all of the time. A feeling of mental well-being may ebb and flow in each of us — something like the movements of the ocean. Some people are like quiet, peaceful waters with only an occasional squall. Others resemble choppy waters with intermittent periods of quiescence and storm. Still others are caught in perpetual confusion or depression, des-

---

°The Christian Counseling Center, 35 South Raymond Avenue, Pasadena, California.

perately trying to find hope and serenity. Somewhere between these extremes you and I, and all others fit in. The
great differences in human personalities, physical attributes,
and experiences, produce an endless variety of emotional
and mental conditions.

Try as we may to tuck our disturbances neatly into pre-
cise clinical categories, we are never too successful. People
are, and always will be, individuals. They are not merely
numbers, or psychological classifications, that are the prey of
the calculating minds and fingers of uniformed researchers.

Take "Aunt Mary," for example. A sociopathic deviate?
Yes and no, but preferably just Aunt Mary. True, she *does* do
some rather strange things, but she's been that way a long
time, and we've gotten used to her. And all the psychological titles seem to fall a little short in getting across what
Aunt Mary is really like.

I suppose we are all just a little like Aunt Mary. Psychologists could put labels of some kind on all of us occasionally, and they might fit rather well. This is true because
people with severe emotional or mental problems are usually
not so different from us in *kind* as they are in *amount*. Their
feelings are like ours except their feelings may be more exaggerated. Too, emotionally disturbed people usually have
less resiliency and "bounce back" more slowly, at least during the time they are feeling at their worst.

Perhaps you have noticed people who have stepped
across the line of healthy thoughts and emotions, into feelings which they can neither control or understand. Yet their
friends or relatives may not realize that such people are
really sick. Each month I receive scores of letters from people who describe a "hateful" or "ornery" relative or neighbor,
without suspecting that the person is desperately in need of
professional help. The following letter points up the fact
very clearly:

"I have an older sister whom I can't understand. She has
always been very mean to my brother and me for as long as we
both can remember. For example, early in her life she would

bite us if we ran home from school ahead of her. We often had black and blue marks on us.

"Now, as an adult, she has almost ruined my life. It used to take me a week to get over my visits home, because she was so mean to my fine parents with whom she lived. She always bossed them around. The last visit I cried to God in prayer that He would break her stony heart, no matter what the cost. Two months after I had asked God to work in her heart, both parents passed away.

"Now, five years later, she lives alone in the family house. When she walks down the street she looks like a fashionable society woman. But not at home! She keeps every piece of paper. She saves empty pickle jars, tin pie plates, paper food containers, paper bags and newspapers. She never washes a dish or spoon. Silverware is corroded with food on it. All pie plates are filthy and heaped over her kitchen table. Dust is on it all.

"Her bed is full of papers. All rooms are littered. Furniture is piled high. Bureaus are a mess on top and drawers all jumbled. Her quilts are on the floor among the litter and she lies on the edge of her paper-littered bed, no sheets, no pillow cases, no quilts used. Her house is filthy.

"What is wrong with such a person? She treats my brother and me terribly. We try to be kind by doing things for her but she soon forgets that we have done anything at all, and is meaner.

"My husband says it's time for me to forget her and let her stew in her own brew. I believe he is right and I intend to stay out of her life except to pray for her salvation.

"When she has money, she buys beautiful gifts for her friends or the men folk in my family. She has never liked her occupation and never held out long on any job.

"My sons hate to see her come. She is so loud-mouthed and bossy to them and to me. All I do is wrong. She treats me like a two-year-old in front of my boys and husband. She gets angry because I don't lend her money.

"I believe I should have her stay out of my home for our family's sake, and I should stay away from her and sever all communication with her including greeting cards for birthdays. Can such a person be helped?"

The answer to this last question is, "Yes, such people can be helped." But most of them need more than our little speeches or quick advice. They need professional help.

With systematic study and psychological evaluation, the well-trained psychologist or psychiatrist can come to understand why a person has taken such a deviate path. Armed with this information, the therapist can begin counseling sessions which culminate in rehabilitation.

What causes a person to become emotionally or mentally ill?

This is like asking the final score of a baseball game at only the sixth inning. It is impossible to give a full, accurate answer because, as yet, the information is not all in. The same is true of emotional and mental problems. We can't give *all* the reasons because we don't have access to them.

But we do have some understanding. We know, for example, that when human beings are deprived of basic emotional needs throughout their early years, they are almost sure to have trouble later on.

The following letter is from a young married woman who became mentally ill. After several months of therapy, she mustered up enough courage to write her parents. This remarkable confession shows what happens to a child when everything in life comes before real love and affection.

"Dear Mother and Dad:

"Since I was a small child, I have had feelings of hate, and not belonging. No, you never knew how I felt. I tried to get it across to you in actions, but I never expressed it in words. In your eyes I was just a rebellious kid, so I felt I should not add to your thoughts by telling you my true feelings. And, after all, we were one of the strongest Christian families in the church and there was supposed to have been only love in our home.

"There was a time when I wanted your love and companionship, but it seemed that other things came first with you two. When I found that I couldn't get the love I needed, I decided to forget you. If you didn't need me or want me, why should I love you? So I became independent of you except financially. As far as I was concerned, you weren't even my parents. Oh yes, you were there, but you weren't making our house a home — to me it was an empty house.

"I have had no feeling for you since I was about twelve.

I couldn't understand, nor can I yet, how you could think that I was just rebellious by nature, and that you had nothing to do with it. Also, how could you think that I loved you?

"You were so concerned with supplying the material needs and teaching me things that would be helpful when I was grown up, that you overlooked the real needs that I had at the time. If I wanted sympathy, you felt you would spoil me, so you'd give me a lecture on facing life and disappointments. If I wanted love, it just didn't seem to be there. Every moment had to count in preparing me for future life. But the present always went begging.

"Now maybe you will understand why I can't accept your love today and why I can't give you any love yet. It's hard to love someone you've hated for so many years. Sometimes I have wanted to love someone so badly I thought I couldn't stand it. I yearned to have the security of acceptance and the warmth of love. But I finally got over that, and now love is completely out of my life — both in giving and receiving.

"Today I want to love you, because you are my parents, but it is hard and confusing. The Lord is taking away my feelings of hate, also my wanting to hurt you with words. I know that He will not leave this problem unfinished. In time, I think He will give me love for you. It will take time because I still have a 'don't touch me' attitude, and a feeling of indifference toward you. It is hard to accept you and your love because you had to be told to do it. I keep wondering, 'Is it real?' You can rest assured that when I finally do show love for you it will be the real thing. But it will take a while, so please be patient and try to understand that I would like to accept you now, but I just can't!"

This young woman's parents, both evangelical Christians, were shocked when they read the letter. In fact, this was the first real communication they had received from the girl (either written or verbal) for some time. As far as they knew, they had done their best for their daughter and they were in no way responsible for her mental illness. Yet they had not given her *themselves, their love*. They had "trained her for the future," but they had not given the necessary day-by-day affection.

There are many such parents. They have given little or no thought to what they are doing to their children, until they come to visit them years later in a mental hospital. You have often read the Scripture, "Train up a child in the way he should go: and when he is old, he will not depart from it" (Proverbs 22:6). This is a very comforting verse. It assures parents that if they do train up a child in the way that he should go that these patterns of living will become well-established in his life and, indeed, difficult to change. But the verse is not so comforting when you look at the other aspect of it. The other side of the verse implies that if wrong patterns are developed in childhood, they, too, will be difficult to change — and therapists everywhere know this.

The emotional problems that plague most people are small ones. Persistent, but small. They nag away at your joys and happiness and leave you a little upset much of the time. But I have learned from the many who write our office each month that, while small problems are a source of irritation and unpleasantness, people often have large problems that are truly disabling. I would like to invite you to step into my office for a few minutes and meet several women who are plagued by emotional and mental problems. You will find that in most ways they are much like yourself. The big difference is, their problems have become so severe that they are no longer able to function well at home and in the community. As you meet each one and hear her story, try to peek behind the mask of her outward life to discover the real causes of her problem. When you have done that, you will want to consider how each might be brought back to a state of healthy, happy living.

Marie is a compulsive eater.

Marie is unable to curb her eating. Although she is a Christian, she feels defeated. Moreover, she is a poor testimony to her unsaved husband.

"I am a born-again Christian, but I am thoroughly mixed up. I weigh much over 200 pounds. I went to see a medical doctor, and he gave me some pills. I have taken them, but I always gain back what I lose, plus more and more. So I do not feel medicine is the answer.

"My husband is unsaved, but he feels that if the Holy

Spirit lives in me, I would obey the Bible. He quotes about the glutton, and the taking of a knife to your throat if you're a person given to appetite. I have sent in for prayer requests, been prayed for — well I can write no more because I feel defeated."

There are various causes of over-eating. A person who is working too hard may eat more than she should to overcome fatigue. Another person may have a glandular imbalance which causes her to become overweight. Still another may eat excessively because she has experienced unusual grief or disappointment. Thus she gains some immediate satisfaction through the tasting of food. Another woman may over-eat because she is bored. Life offers no challenge for her, so "snacking" becomes a point of interest to break the routine monotony of her life. There are a host of disturbing conditions which often produce sufficient discontent and anxiety to cause a person to turn to food for temporary comfort and relief. Yet studies reveal that many compulsive eaters have basic emotional needs which were never adequately met. An emotional deprivation in childhood may take the form of an oral need. This is often true when there have been unsatisfactory relationships with parents or parent substitutes. This causes a conflict and the whole process becomes somatogenisized, that is, it shows itself in physical ailments or complaints. In other words, when an actual emotional need is not met, a person adopts a physical means of obtaining what he has not experienced emotionally. Eating is one of the resolutions to this type of conflict. Marie may be, in essence, consuming food as a substitute for the fulfillment of her emotional needs.

Physicians often prescribe medication to help curb this appetite while they also recommend diets. But these methods seldom offer permanent solutions. What is more, as the oral need is denied, another symptom is likely to develop.

The best means of dealing with the problem is an actual resolution of the basic conflict. Through professional counseling, one's early life is brought to light and some of the conflictual areas are talked out. The Christian counselor also presents God in all His fatherly love and glory. If the person is able to assimilate the valid concept that God is a loving, forgiving Father, the problem is often resolved. When the counselee comes to a deeper understanding of the love of God personally, His overwhelming love can fulfill the neglected need for affection.

Psychological testing and clinical interviews often indicate that a person like Marie has a very poor self-concept. Sometimes compulsive eating represents a form of withdrawal from society. One may compensate by satisfying his needs on a physical level (eating). This is a rather circular process in which the person becomes defeated in his life circumstances. In other words, the person eats to escape frustration and anxiety, and by eating he becomes obese. Hence, he weakens an already inadequate self-concept.

A compulsive eater needs therapy. Being a Christian and growing in the Lord also helps immensely. But simply listening to a sermon is not adequate. The person should experience a positive relationship with a Christian therapist who can lead him to an understanding of his inner feelings as well as to a closer walk with Christ.

Janice is beset by evil thoughts.

This letter is from a Christian mother who is concerned about her grown daughter. The young woman is emotionally distressed and plagued with evil thoughts.

"All through school, our daughter was an honor student, but she had a nervous breakdown in the tenth grade. She was always very shy and timid, and through the years she has had serious problems.

"She is now twenty-eight years old and has had numerous shock treatments. She has been to different psychiatrists, and has taken many of the new drugs until the limit of the prescriptions has been reached. As soon as their effectiveness wears off, her condition returns to its former state.

"We are Christians and she has been baptized, but she does not read her Bible. She says she cannot understand it. She does not like religious music because she says it makes her feel guilty. She tells me that she is tormented by bad thoughts and does not wish to see anyone because she is afraid they will see that she does not like them. She doesn't even want to ride past the homes of anyone she knows for fear they will see her, and know that she has evil thoughts about them.

"It is an awful existence. She always looks out of the windows in every direction before she will go outside. If I have callers she goes to her room and weeps. She has almost ruined her eyes by crying.

"The last doctor we had wanted to send her to our local hospital, and give her heavy doses of some new drugs. However, he would not guarantee that she would not suffer a permanent heart injury or paralysis agitans (shaking palsy), so we would not consent. If those drugs wear off, it would be the same thing.

"She tells me that she is ashamed to tell the doctors her thoughts, that sex matters are troubling her. We never talked to her about sex because she didn't bring up the subject. A lady doctor explained menstruation to her. She is a very particular person, keeping her room immaculate, and is very methodical. She and I just can't seem to get along. She says I make her sick."

It is significant that Janice has been emotionally ill for a long time. The severity of the illness and its long duration would tend to negate her becoming an honor student unless she had been pushed by her parents.

The mother mentions that the girl has evil thoughts about everyone. The fact that she feels guilty and has evil thoughts suggests that she has been able to suppress her evil thoughts until she was fifteen years old in the tenth grade. If so, the repression of the thoughts and the guilt over the thoughts undoubtedly caused more anxiety than her personality could tolerate. Consequently, this could have been partially responsible for a nervous breakdown.

Now she is unable to face people because she has evil thoughts about them. In many cases the evil thoughts originate in reference to parents due to strong feelings of hate, coupled with lack of communication. In the case of Janice, the intense feelings have now been generalized to include much of society.

The girl also mentions that she has sex problems which

are troubling her. The parents may have had a certain piety in which realistic problems of children were taboo, causing feelings of guilt about natural inclinations and curiosities. As a result, she may have had to repress all of her questions or feelings about sex. Yet, they persisted internally.

It may even have been that the parents were rather rigid people who would not tolerate normal childhood expressions. Instead, they may have tried to mold the girl's behavior early in life into an adult pattern which she was incapable of accepting. If this was the case, she may have been given more criticism than sincere understanding. Today, all of her outward expressions are inhibited and repressed.

Janice does not care to read her Bible or to have anything to do with religious matters. They may symbolize her early childhood training in reference to her parents. She may be baptized, but unsaved, and she may have guilt feelings about the Word. Furthermore, her disturbance is too great to concentrate on reading.

Since her mother only seems to feed into her pathology, hospitalization would have the advantage of separating her from her mother. This girl would probably make the best progress if she could be seen by an interested and considerate Christian therapist. He could bring spiritual truths to bear when appropriate. With adequate care she may be able to take her place again in society.

Madge has a compulsion to perform dangerous acts.

Madge writes of her compulsion to touch electrical outlets and fixtures. She does not understand why she has this uncontrollable urge, but she knows that she needs help.

"My problem is this: I have compulsions to touch electrical outlets and fixtures with wet hands. This started right after we moved to the city from the country about two months ago.

"Since this is dangerous, I know I must overcome it. I wonder if you have any information on a problem such as this. I have prayed about it, but it seems to be getting worse."

Undoubtedly there are other symptoms not mentioned which would indicate that Madge has self-destructive tendencies. These are usually the result of a certain amount of hostility directed toward oneself. Many times it is brought about by a pronounced feeling of guilt over a severe emotional conflict in childhood.

In her letter, Madge uses the word "compulsion," which we know is a response to an impulse that is largely unconscious. Although she may suppress the desire to harm herself, she cannot actually control it.

Interestingly enough, Madge's compulsions began after she moved from the country to the city. It is possible that something about the move brought to consciousness the impulse to injure herself. In therapy this would be explored thoroughly, as it is quite possible that she may feel some strong attachments to the country and resent being taken away. She may be frightened of city life, feeling insecure among crowds of people. Another phobic reaction might be that being among people makes her lose her identity or brings about some other reaction.

Many times a self-destructive compulsion is the result of inner hostilities directed toward someone else, or perhaps to one or both parents. When a person does not strike out at others, pent-up feelings of anger and resentment are then directed back toward oneself. Since these feelings are obscured in the subconscious, they may give rise to compulsion. What she understands is that she has a strong urge to hurt herself. She also has enough insight to realize that the symptom is severe enough to seek professional help.

Madge makes no mention of having ever accepted Christ as her Saviour. A Christian counselor will have the opportunity to tell her of the love of God and to make sure she understands the forgiveness offered her through Christ.

Annette is concerned about frequent blushing.

The following letter is from a woman who is bothered by constant blushing. The problem is causing her so much distress that she wonders if she might be losing her mind.

"Did you ever hear of a married woman (with six children) blushing all the time? I have always blushed ever since I was a child, but now it is getting to the place where I am afraid to talk to anyone for fear of turning red.

"I teach a fine class of junior girls in Sunday school and I find myself blushing if I even make a little mistake in talking. I am afraid to speak up in our teachers' meetings, for when I do say something, I can feel I am turning crimson. When my husband teases me in front of people, especially relatives or in-laws, I blush. This thing is beginning to affect my Christian testimony, for I am beginning to draw into a shell and not talk for fear of blushing.

"Is my mind going? Is there any help for a problem like this?"

The common psychological definition for blushing is an internal slap in the face. It dynamically represents a growing sense of insecurity. Annette is afraid she will expose her feelings whether she wants to or not.

Severe blushing is nature's way of alerting a person to feelings that are deeply rooted but have largely been repressed. These feelings are attempting to become conscious and seek expression. She blushes and becomes more withdrawn from people, and because she is withdrawn she is less able to express herself. This leads to frequent and more pronounced blushing. It is as though feelings that have long been buried or handled by an inadequate control system are now threatening to become conscious.

Some people blush because they are not able to express themselves. They usually feel embarrassed, then blush. A person may also become embarrassed because he feels that he has done something wrong and it is obvious to others. Annette probably has no actual awareness of why the feeling exists. Nevertheless, the feeling alerts the autonomic nervous system and the blushing is set up. Sometimes just a simple cue or word will set up this mechanism. A word which touches on some significant, dynamic, unconscious material evokes the response. Women who do not cry easily often tend to have a pronounced reddening, particularly around the face and neck.

Inferiority feelings may also inaugurate blushing. People

who have persistently been the brunt of ridicule and criticism are likely to blush. Children who do not succeed and are constantly reminded of their failures sometimes develop this habit. Overcritical parents often cause their children to feel embarrassed if they do not meet demands of perfection. In Annette's case, her husband's teasing may trigger some hidden feelings of her childhood, and blushing is the means by which they come to the front.

Annette should find some person in whom she has confidence and with whom she can share her feelings. The person should be professionally-trained or at least a sympathetic listener. By ventilating her feelings and finding the true causes of them she can obtain considerable relief and develop new attitudes.

Although Annette is a Sunday school teacher, she may well benefit from spiritual help. Nothing makes a person more assured and confident than knowing his position in Christ. As this is considered Annette may improve considerably.

Pauline does not trust men.

After much urging by a friend, Pauline, a Christian woman, went to see a Christian psychologist. The first session was spent in trying to ascertain the nature of her problem. Pauline, however, was extremely reluctant to talk. She had four children who were all failing in school. The counselor found no evidence to indicate that an organic condition might exist for all four, and he suspected that the children's lack of success in school was probably related to some type of home problem. Pauline seemed unusually defensive and attempted to discount her own role in the family. Several months earlier she had gone to see a minister. However, she went to see him only four times, stating that because he was a man, she did not think he could actually understand her problem. Pauline was unhappy. She felt that something had to be done for the children. "Would it be advisable to bring them in to the psychologist?" she wondered. The counselor agreed that this might be a possibility, but that they would want to think of the diffi-

culty in terms of a *family problem*. She was then encouraged
to come back for another visit.

Pauline was nearly a half hour late for her second appointment. It was not difficult to realize that she came reluctantly. During this session the psychologist was quite
direct and told her that he thought the problem was largely
her own, and had been with her for some years.

Pauline immediately broke into tears and confessed that
she had had emotional problems as long as she could remember. The remainder of the session was spent in reassuring
her that she could be helped. She left, stating she still felt
that a man could not really help her. The counselor then
wondered whether it would be best to refer her to a woman
psychologist on the staff. However, he felt that the problem
lay largely in reference to the male figure, and that this
might be the best grounds on which to work it out.

Pauline appeared late for her third interview, but a little more in control of her depression. She had determined
that she would come to the session and thereby achieve a
personal victory. The psychologist praised her for her effort.
He also casually suggested that a psychological test might
be of benefit in order to evaluate her personality structure.
She immediately became defensive, so the therapist dropped
the subject. They then talked about her children, her husband, and current circumstances in the home. Little by little
she became more comfortable in expressing her feelings.
The therapist said little, only occasionally punctuating the
conversation with a few complimentary remarks. She wondered how much longer she had to come, since the three
sessions had not made her feel any better. In fact, she said
she felt even more depressed at times. The counselor told
her that therapy would probably be a long-term process,
because her problem was deep and had been accumulating
for many years. She left somewhat discouraged but said she
would return.

Pauline arrived promptly for the fourth session, which
again was interpreted to her as an encouraging sign. She
was still hesitant and defensive during the first part of the
hour and it took all the efforts the counselor could muster

to encourage her to talk. She generalized a great deal about her situation; then finally, at one point, while talking about her husband, she unconsciously slipped and called him "father." This, in addition to some other statements she had dropped, gave the psychologist a clue that perhaps one of the reasons she felt as she did was that she had married someone much like her father. She openly stated that this was probably true — her husband was "just like her father." She went on to say that one of the biggest sources of irritation was the fact that she was unable to communicate with her husband. The counselor again suggested that this might be true also in her father relationships. At this point the therapy hour was near an end, and it was undoubtedly best, because she was becoming extremely upset.

Pauline did not show up for the fifth session, nor did she notify the office. After missing the sixth and seventh appointments, the therapist phoned her. She was reluctant to talk, but did say that there was something about the therapist that upset her, and she could not feel comfortable talking to him. With some encouragement, she finally consented to come back for one session. This, as was proved later, was to be an interesting interview.

A little before the appointment time, Pauline arrived and sat nervously in her chair in the reception room. She looked as though she were ready to cry. When she came into the office she again was determined not to reveal any of her thoughts and feelings. The session was opened with a word of prayer, asking God's help. The first ten minutes or so were spent attempting to encourage Pauline to talk about herself. Finally, in desperation, she broke down and cried. Sobbingly, she stated that she had never met anyone like the therapist. All men had been cruel to her, she said, particularly her father and her husband. She had never felt that men had any interest in her and did not care if she lived or died. Pauline talked continually the rest of the period. Her father, she said, was an overly-critical and rigid person who demanded adherence in terms of duty and not in love. Her early identification with her father was that of a taskmaster who demanded strict conformity to his every whim. But he did not give his child love. Although the Scriptures clearly instruct fathers not to provoke their children to wrath, he did just the opposite. After years of cruel treatment, Pauline had built up much resentment and hostility toward men figures and felt that they were all against her. During childhood and throughout marriage she had known nothing else. She had married a man who was a prototype of her father. She had used the children as a scapegoat for her own problems, and had worked out her hostility on them. She unconsciously felt she couldn't fight back against a powerful, sadistic male figure. In working with the therapist and finding that she could express herself in a permissive and sympathetic way, a new avenue of expression began to open to her.

Even though Pauline began to feel that she could talk about herself to a man who appeared to be a more loving figure than she had known, she still had to run away during several of the first scheduled visits. Her way of perceiving men in general had been undermined. Consequently, when she met a man who was not symbolically cruel and sadistic to her, she still had to run away.

Pauline still had a long way to go in reformulating a whole new theory about men. She did find, however, that as she was able to express herself, her hostility, which was actually misplaced and directed toward the children, began to decrease. She was able to work out her feelings of anger, frustration and rejection with the therapist. He also introduced the fact that even though she could never have complete confidence in people, that she could always place unlimited trust in God. As she discussed this truth, she gained insight and strength, and was soon on her way to a more meaningful, happy life.

Marian is suffering from depression.

Like many others, the writer of this letter is seriously depressed. She is the mother of four young children and has very little understanding of her problem.

"My main problem is being depressed. Sometimes I think I must really be ill to feel so blue all the time.

"Ever since I became pregnant with my fourth child I

haven't enjoyed the children at all. I used to take them for walks; but I just can't seem to fit it in anymore. What's more, I feel hateful. I become so angry and frustrated I can't even think straight.

"Just yesterday I became so angry with my oldest daughter who is six, that I told her I couldn't stand her, that she made me sick, and that she should shut her ugly mouth. I know it's wrong. I constantly read Christian literature for help and yet I'm getting worse.

"When I learned I was pregnant for the third time, I had a bad emotional problem. I was so upset that all my resentment came back stronger than ever.

"This last baby screams all the time, even when he eats. The doctor says he's healthy. I wonder why God gave him to me just when I was beginning to appreciate the others.

"I think it would help if I knew a wonderful Christian woman who could come once a week and pray with me, one with whom I could confide my daily upsets. We could pray about them together. Sometimes I feel I can't stand it any more. I think, 'What kind of fears will these poor children have as they grow up?' Yet the daily upsets pile high, and I can't read or pray them off. They just keep happening. I know I'm more depressed than is healthy, *very much so*. I even doubt God and say, 'Why do You let this happen?'

"It's more than I'm able to bear."

Depression is a symptom of deep emotional problems. Such illness is usually caused by repressed hostility. This is probably true of Marian. The children apparently represent her mounting responsibility and a loss of personal freedom. She is working out this hostility on her children.

A person's physical condition can have a marked influence upon his emotional outlook. Therefore, medical counsel should be sought when one experiences severe feelings of depression. Marian, who has four young children, may not be in good physical health. This would contribute greatly to her emotional condition.

The dynamics here may also suggest a woman who wants to depend upon other people. Instead, she is forced into the role of actually being the one on whom the children are dependent. Naturally, this threatens her. She feels that God should miraculously keep her from having children in spite of the fact that she has normal sex relations, then becomes pregnant. This is a rather misdirected and self-denying perception. In her illness she blames the Lord, her Heavenly Father, for allowing things to happen to her which she could actually control. She is disappointed that God does not act as a birth control agent for her. Now that she finds herself in a situation which requires more of her time and attention, she feels unable to cope with it.

She is actually shifting the responsibility and blame toward God. But since He isn't "working in her behalf," she is possibly denying His existence. This adds up to an unstable person. Her illness is becoming more pronounced and she is probably regressing to a more infantile state of assessing her situation.

The repressed anxiety is now breaking through and is directly proportional to the amount of responsibility that she feels. From her resentment toward God it is suggested that the hostility may have originated in reference to her father. It is altogether possible that he was a strong figure on whom she depended for emotional security. In becoming a Christian she may have transferred some of this dependency to God the Father. This is not uncommon, because many people tend to think of God as they think of their own earthly father. If one's father is a gentle person, it is easy to think of God as having gentle attributes. If, on the other hand, one's father is strict and judicial, it is difficult to think of God as being loving and forgiving.

Marian feels that it would help if a Christian woman could come once a week to pray with her and to talk about her daily upsets. This, of course, is an excellent idea. A stable, godly woman could encourage Marian to talk, thereby relieving her tensions. Also, some insight might be gained. In addition, the comfort and instruction of the Word would far outstrip any other remedy.

But there is also a word of warning to the pastor or Christian woman who *does* go on this weekly mission. Marian's need for someone to lean on is so overwhelming that she would probably not be a pleasant person to talk to. She may attach herself so closely that it would be difficult for the other person to get away. Her constant talking, caused by her deep frustration, may run anyone off after the first visit.

Hostility feelings need understanding. The feelings of hate, resentment and anger fall into two general categories. One includes those hostile feelings that come quickly to mind when a person thinks of certain situations that irritate him. The other category includes those hostile feelings which lie buried deep in the subconscious and are not readily brought to mind. Many are so repressed as to require deep therapy to uncover them. Although they are on an unconscious level, they have a way of influencing attitudes, moods and emotional stability.

Most people who suffer from depression have had a lack of meaningful love in their childhood. Therefore, a serious study of God's love as revealed in the Bible is helpful. The book of First John is excellent to read through in one sitting, and repeatedly. First Corinthians 13, Romans 8, John 14 and 15, and the book of Ephesians are also especially beneficial.

Marian needs help from a competent Christian counselor who can skillfully lead her to self-understanding and a deeper trust in the Lord.

Elsie is a compulsive reader.

Elsie feels compelled to read almost continually. Yet she knows that it consumes too much time and feels it is a sin before God. She does not understand the causes of her problem.

"On one of your radio broadcasts you read a letter from a wife bound to reading. I have a queer problem. *I have to read all day.* Mostly it is Gospel material I pore over, although *Reader's Digest* and catalogs take my time also. I could blame some of my lethargy, lack of enthusiasm, laziness or whatever, to a medical background of thyroid and a mild past polio condition. I am instructed to take thyroid, digitalis and antihistamine for allergy.

"However, I feel it surely must be sin. Have you anything to advise on how to conquer this? I want completely to glorify my Saviour and win souls. But my home is a very poor witness.

I'm not consistent with the children, either, *and my home is not a little bit of Heaven*. I fear I will be found wanting when He comes for His own.

"Much strength is lost on fighting this besetting sin. There is a loss of prayer power and peace of mind that He's promised. This awful mood is with me almost constantly and so I am filled with self.

"My doctor is very thorough but *unsaved*. So I cannot, for his soul's sake, unburden my confusion and dilemma. I have witnessed my belief to him and I'm afraid for him to know that I have no power.

"I have lost some of my faith in my pastor because he has spoken of things revealed to him, so I cannot go to him. Besides, he only says, 'You'll not be perfect while here.'

"What I want is power over Satan and circumstance — knowledge to know how to accept or reject my plight — to be content. But I have to read day and night."

The basis of compulsive reading is actually an attempt to avoid reality. It is usually a symptom of an unconscious desire to withdraw or escape. For one reason or another a person feels that he cannot relate to others on a social basis, so he escapes into the printed page. This fantasy life is much like daydreaming or extreme night dreaming. Some problem in Elsie's life has forced her to seek escape from reality and she has adopted this particular symptom.

Another motivation for compulsive reading is an attempt to overcome feelings of inferiority. The person tends to gain extensive knowledge from written material so that he can "be ahead of other people." Such a person is usually insecure and lacks self-assurance.

Compulsive reading is also a defensive operation. That is, when one cannot handle emotional problems he converts the problem into an intellectual consideration. Thereby the importance of dealing with any problem emotionally is minimized and an intellectualization process sets in. Usually a compulsive reader will have a very poor self-concept. Thinking he is unworthy, he withdraws into another life through books.

Elsie reads Christian literature and says she wants to be a dedicated Christian. Therapy is recommended, but it will be difficult for her to formulate a workable relation with the therapist. She is probably frightened of social situations and is somewhat withdrawn. The therapist will want to reassure Elsie that the problem is a common emotional reaction to some type of deep seated problem. She should be assured also that this is not necessarily sinful, but rather, a symptom of an emotional problem. Therefore she does not have to feel defeated. (Christians with emotional problems often feel even greater defeat because they believe in some way they must be sinning.) It should be explained to Elsie that she is not necessarily committing a sin; rather, she is acting out a maladjustment.

If she has no social outlets it would be advisable for her to pursue such. Christian activities would be helpful. The more she involves herself socially, the less need she will feel for excessive reading. What residuals there may be of this compulsion could be channeled into reading to help others.

Shirley's frigidity is causing her husband concern.

Shirley and her husband have an unsatisfactory sex life. The husband wants help for his wife.

"We are home missionaries with two children, and have been married for six years. We have peace within our home on most things except our sexual relations. My wife's desires are almost nil.

"What could lead us to a more happy, contented life in this respect?

"Perhaps one of the reasons for this is that when my wife was a child, her mother instilled in her mind that all sex was wrong and to be avoided.

"If you can give us some information that would lead us to a fuller and more contented life, we would certainly appreciate it."

It is interesting that the husband says they get along quite well in most ways except sexually. Marital problems usually arise when there is trouble in one area and it is generalized to others. For example, problems of finances, difficulties with in-laws, misunderstandings over children, and other conflicts may reveal themselves in unsatisfactory sex relations. Although this may be true of Shirley and her husband, statements in the letter indicate that this is not necessarily the case.

Evidently, Shirley's parents saw sex in a very negative way, making her feel guilty about heterosexual relationships. This fact in itself is sufficient to cause Shirley to feel as she does today. If she could sit down with a Christian counselor for several sessions and discuss the causes of her feelings, she would eventually develop new attitudes and be able to respond normally to her husband. There are many aspects of the problem which have not been mentioned in this brief letter, and they need to be carefully considered. *

Frigidity on the part of a wife sometimes reflects an early childhood conflict with her father. When communication between father and daughter is noticeably impaired for a long period of time, the reaction will sometimes be generalized to matters of sex. In such instances, the girl becomes afraid of men in general, and later in marriage is unable to enter into intimate relationships with her husband. Fortunately Shirley and her husband are Christians and have common ground on which they can express their feelings and achieve a good adjustment. In addition to counseling sessions, the couple would no doubt benefit from literature on the causes of frigidity. As they gain deeper insights into their problem, they will be able to resolve it.

Eleanor, a compulsive liar, is severely emotionally disturbed.

The writer of this letter is suffering from emotional illness. She feels that she is unloved and that no one is concerned about her.

"Five years ago my family doctor suggested I have counseling with a pastor about my emotional problems. I did for awhile; then I quit, vastly improved. But the pastor left and I again became terribly confused.

"Now I am annoyed. I lied to my counselor because I am

---

*For a further discussion of sex problems, see Chapter 11, Sex Problems in Marriage.

a liar by nature. I wasted his time. But is there such a thing as a hypochondriac who is emotionally ill?

"I went to my session with words, words and more words, only to leave more annoyed for not telling the truth or for not accomplishing anything. I always seem to be pretending. I am a shallow, melodramatic type of person. I have a different personality for each friend or situation. I am like a switchboard, where I plug into the necessary type person.

"I am always trying to be the center of attention. I am self-centered. I get so involved in my own feeling or lack of feeling that I don't function properly. I have a terrible longing to be loved or cared for by someone. This has caused me a lot of turmoil because I have not always been able to use good judgment in trying to find someone to love me. I tend to be a fickle, flirty type of person. But even worse, I keep telling people all my problems, even though this is degrading. I am disgusted with myself for doing it. Am I trying to get pity or love? Why can't I shut up?

"I have been married nine years and we have four children. They are four children in need of a good mother. My husband would also profit if I could be a different sincere person. I have a loving father — weak, but loving — who lives some distance away. I either adore him or hate him. I have four brothers and sisters who have always had pugnacious attitudes toward me. But I am lost without them.

"I am an active church member, a half-hearted gardener and a tired sewer. I read a lot, but I change hobbies weekly. I've tried every possible thing to be interested in. Nothing helps. I still feel empty and alone. Fear controls my life, fear of not being accepted. Can you help me to be a person who could be an honest homemaker and a good partner in marriage, a true friend? Please!"

Eleanor is evidently a very disturbed person and in all probability has a characterological disorder. The basis of the problem, namely the ambivalence that she feels, is where her emotions of love and hate have existed and are continuing to exist simultaneously.

There is little or no stability in her life because there are no well-developed and ingrained love relationships with anyone. She is simply tossed to and fro and uses words as a wedge for acceptance as well as an instrument of not becoming involved with people. She also employs them as a defense against being overwhelmed by situations.

Eleanor seems to be a compulsive liar, which probably represents a great measure of insecurity. As indicated in the letter, her father is most likely a weak and passive personality who did not serve as an adequate male figure in her childhood. Her resentment of her mother is suggested by the conspicuous absence of any mention whatsoever. In all possibility, neither parent gave her much love, nor were they the kind of parents on whom she could depend. She also has ambivalent feelings toward her brothers and sisters. She feels they do not accept her, therefore she resents them. At the same time she seems dependent upon them. As a result, she has become rather fixated and limited in her capacities for emotional response to others. She is confused by people, not knowing how to relate to them because she does not understand the fuller nuances of the emotions of others. This is due to her own emotional deprivation. She was never given an emotional gauge by which to judge how she felt about people and how others felt about her. Complicating this is her ambivalence between love and hate. She does not fully understand a complete love relationship and consequently feels hostile because she does not even understand the dependency needs that she feels. It is unfortunate that she was not saved and taught in the Word at an early age. An emotional deprivation in the home can sometimes be met in the church if the wonderful love of God is preached and if Christian friends demonstrate God's love.

This is a pathetic case and one that represents a difficult task for a therapist. The reason for this is that if Eleanor does become involved in a transference relationship (an affectionate or hostile reaction) with the therapist, she may develop hostility toward him because she feels she cannot depend on him, not having been able to depend on anyone up to the present time. She also feels that there is something vague about such concepts as "love," which she cannot understand. Consequently, she feels anxious about discussing these terms. This is particularly exemplified in one of her statements about her father: "I either adore him or hate him." At first it may be difficult to talk to her about Christ dying for her sin, because she doesn't understand love. Eleanor vacillates from dependency to independency. She wants to depend on a person but is afraid to do so. As a result, she has developed some mechanisms which she feels will give her a certain amount of independence. This again is indicated in the fact that she wants attention, while at the same time not wanting to be actually emotionally involved with others.

This woman should definitely receive intensive psychiatric care. If the therapist is well-trained, as well as being a born-again Christian, Eleanor should be able to make great strides toward a better adjustment in life.

Terry has guilt feelings about sexual promiscuity.

Not long ago I received a letter from a woman who told of her sexual promiscuity and the resultant severe feelings of guilt. She claimed that she was presently married to a good Christian man and everything was going along well in their home. She confided, however, that earlier in their married life she became intimate with several men and even accepted money from them. Now she is disturbed and depressed and is seeking counsel. She stated that for the last eighteen months she has had no relations with other men and is devoted to her husband. She also said that she has been convinced from hearing Christian radio programs that her sexual relationships were immoral and she is now feeling very guilty. She said that although she now feels closer to God, she also feels correspondingly guilty.

Certainly, as she gets closer to God, she will become more aware of her shortcomings and sin. This woman is probably under deep conviction relating to her adultery and is becoming disturbed over it. She did not mention whether she was a believer in the Lord Jesus Christ. Indeed He can forgive sin, any sin, and is willing to do so. She is probably becoming much more guilt-oriented as she learns God's standards of righteousness and perfection.

In leading Terry to Christ, a counselor should deal thoroughly with sin, its consequences and its forgiveness through Christ. Sin is a reality and it must be dealt with in a real way. Only the blood of Christ cleanses us from sin. "Forasmuch as ye know that ye were not redeemed with corruptible things, as silver and gold, from your vain conversation received by tradition from your fathers; But with the precious blood of Christ, as of a lamb without blemish and without spot" (I Peter 1:18, 19).

By carefully considering and accepting God's complete forgiveness, and by talking through her feelings, this woman, like many before her, can walk in newness of life and become a radiant Christian.

Betty has a bad temper.

This letter is from Betty who has a bad temper which she feels she has inherited. Since other members of the family have been in mental institutions she is also concerned about her own mental health.

"Why is it that when you want to live a Christian life it seems like so much goes against it? I don't know whether you believe in the stars or not, but I was born in May under 'Taurus the Bull.' I believe at times I live up to it pretty well. I have the temper of a bull at times. Also I let my nerves get the best of me, and I fly to pieces. Violent tempers run on both sides of my family. My husband was also born under this sign and has practically the same makeup.

"About three years ago we adopted two girls. We had been married thirteen years then. I wasn't in favor of them, both because of nerves and my age. I am almost 33 now. My husband thinks I'm silly for these ideas. I had our name in for eight years to adopt a baby. I don't believe in feeling sorry for myself but it seems like I get awfully depressed at times.

"We have been saved for nine years. But my husband doesn't care for church as he did at one time. As a rule, he treats me real well, but he sees very little wrong in the girls. He thinks they can do no wrong.

"When I was a child my own home was not good. My dad was an alcoholic and my mother was sick most of the time and unable to help us. It was bedlam. Several persons from our family have been in mental institutions. Of course I want to stay away from there. I have been to the doctor and he always says its just nerves. I would so much appreciate your counsel."

Temper tantrums are usually functional in nature unless there is a neurological impairment or some other physical problem. Loss of ego controls will permit the outburst of impulsive material. This is when the person feels nervous and unable to control herself.

Betty is evidently becoming more pronounced in temper outbursts as her husband is showing general disinterest in her. She may be jealous, feeling insecure in her relationship with her husband. She undoubtedly sees the two girls as standing in the way of her happiness. Part of her worry is that she will have to be confined in a mental institution as did some of her family. Hence, her primary concern is how to control herself so that she can remain at home and live a happy life.

She is also considering the effect of the stars, and states that she was born under Taurus the Bull and lives up to this since she has such a violent and uncontrollable temper. This sounds rather magical in the sense that the stars can control her behavior. Actually, it is probably a denial of her own ability to control herself and an attempt to attribute the responsibility of her actions to some other source. Her parents may not have encouraged self-control, so she has grown up with the belief that it is permissible to act out uncontrollable temper. In other words, her unstable home environment did not teach adequate control systems. In addition, she had no worthy parental example which she could emulate.

Usually a child lives at an emotional level similar to his parents. If the parent illustrates that it is permissible to have temper tantrums by openly displaying them, the child will pick up the same idea. Betty undoubtedly needs counseling sessions in which she can reformulate and relearn some early childhood experiences. Meditation on the Scriptures and a greater dedication to God would permit the Holy Spirit to do an important work in her life. In addition, she should be evaluated from a medical standpoint to determine if there may be physical bases for her problem.

Bad tempers that "run in families" are usually not inherited, but are passed along because it is permissible to have them, and because certain conflicts and problems have become overwhelming.

Improving Your Own Emotional and Mental Well-Being.

Your emotional and mental well-being is never static. It fluctuates day by day. Over a period of a year or more it may change considerably. This is because you are a dynamic being living in a dynamic environment. Just as physical changes are taking place inside you, so people and conditions are changing around you. All of this interaction affects your emotional health.

Following is an inventory which will help you gain a clearer picture of your own emotional and mental well-being. Read each statement carefully. Then, place a check mark in front of those which you feel you need to improve.

AN INVENTORY OF EMOTIONAL AND MENTAL WELL-BEING

1. *What kind of image do I hold of myself?*
   - I am not overwhelmed by my own emotions — by my fears, anger, love, jealousy or worries.
   - I can usually take life's disappointments in stride.
   - I have a tolerant attitude toward myself as well as others; I can laugh at myself.
   - I neither under-estimate nor over-estimate my abilities.
   - I can accept my own shortcomings.
   - I have a good measure of self-respect.
   - I feel able to deal with most situations that come my way.
   - I get satisfaction from simple, everyday pleasures.

2. *What are my true feelings about others?*
   - I am able to give love and to consider the interests of others.
   - I have personal relationships that are satisfying and lasting.
   - I expect to like and trust others, and take it for granted that others will like and trust me.
   - I respect the many differences I find in people.
   - I do not push people around, nor do I allow myself to be pushed around.
   - I can feel I am part of a group.

• I feel a sense of responsibility to my neighbors and fellow-men.

3. *How do I meet the demands of life?*
   • I do something about my problems as they arise.
   • I accept my just responsibilities.
   • I shape my environment whenever possible, and adjust to it whenever necessary.
   • I plan ahead, but I do not fear the future.
   • I welcome new experiences and new ideas.
   • I make use of my natural capacities.
   • I set realistic goals for myself.
   • I am able to think for myself and make my own decisions.
   • I put my best effort into what I do and get satisfaction from it.

How is your score? If you feel that you need definite improvement, you should ask the Lord to help you. Like many others, you may also profit from seeing a profession-ally-trained Christian counselor.

If you are suffering from poor emotional or mental health, rest assured that you can do something about it. Every day, people with severe emotional problems are re-ceiving professional help and are becoming happy and well-adjusted.

The first step to improvement is to admit that you do have a problem. Since we all have at least some maladjust-ments, it is no disgrace to bring your own difficulty out in the open. A wise person will say, "Yes, my problems have increased beyond the point of my handling them alone. I do need professional help."

The next step is to rule out any possible physical causes. A medical specialist can often discover physical ailments, then begin to treat them. However, if medical doctors are unable to find any physical bases for your symptoms, you should turn to other types of specialists. Many women suf-fering from emotional illness hopefully consult doctor after doctor, failing to achieve the health they so desperately long for.

If your problems do not seem to have a physical basis, you may wish to consult a Christian psychologist or psychia-trist. You may have to do this in spite of advice from family, friends and other well-meaning people who may not under-stand the nature or value of psychological help. I am fre-quently asked, "Just what does a psychologist do when you go to his office?" Such questions are natural inasmuch as most people have not consulted a psychologist and are not sure what procedures are followed. Usually, the Christian psychologist will utilize the initial interview to become acquainted with you and to gain an understanding of your particular problem. During the next session or two he will probably give you psychological tests in order to learn more about your personality structure. These sessions are then followed by counseling, during which time you will come to understand the true causes of your problem, and through full discussion to help eliminate them. The number of ses-sions required differs from person to person. Some people need only a few, others more. The therapy may be somewhat intensive with sessions each day, or it may extend over a longer period with sessions spaced a week apart.

Since you are a spiritual being, you should not overlook the possibility that your problems may actually be caused by unmet spiritual needs. To be sure of your salvation and your continued spiritual development, you may turn to your own pastor or to some other spiritual leader in whom you have confidence. A Christian psychologist would, of course, be able to give you both spiritual and psychological help.° In fact, they are inseparable and should be considered to-gether. Your emotional and mental well-being is important and you should not neglect it. You deserve to be at your best.

°If you wish to write the author directly about professional psycho-logical services, address your correspondence to Box 206, Pasadena, California.

CHAPTER THREE

The Woman Outside the Home

Today, more and more women are leaving the home scene for full-time employment outside the home. This trend began to pick up momentum during World War II when women were "drafted" for defense work. Since then, for many, staying home has become the exception rather than the rule. After working outside the home, one woman said, "I wouldn't give up working for anything in the world."

Much of the world's business is handled by women. Indeed, some of our most brilliant minds in business, government, art, music and education are of the fairer sex. And many miracles of salvation have been wrought in such places as women have witnessed for Christ.

Some people question whether a married woman should *ever* work outside the home. They quote: "That they may teach the young women to be sober, to love their husbands, to love their children, to be discreet, chaste, keepers at home, good, obedient to their own husbands, that the word of God be not blasphemed" (Titus 2:4, 5).

When we take a closer look at this text, we cannot find any directive for a woman to devote herself exclusively to household duties. Nor does the Word say that a woman should *not* work outside the home. The root meaning in the Greek of "keepers at home" is "guardians of the home." It means that a married woman's first responsibility is to her home. She is to make it attractive, take time with the children, help her husband, and be queen in her castle. This is her first obligation. Dr. Groskery puts it this way, "The first duty of a Christian woman is to make her home happy.

Religion gains no honor when home duties are neglected." The classical Greek use of the phrase goes beyond the concept of working outside of the home. It gives the idea that women are not to be "gadabouts," part of every club activity at the expense of God-given home obligations.

God can honor women who work outside the home, if they are in His will. Take, for example, the experience of Paul and Silas, meeting a business woman as they preached the Gospel in and around Philippi: "And on the sabbath day we went outside the (city's) gate to the bank of the river, where we supposed there was (an accustomed) place of prayer, and we sat down and addressed the women who had assembled there. One of those who listened to us was a woman named Lydia, from the city of Thyatira, a dealer in fabrics dyed in purple. She was (already) a worshiper of God, and the Lord opened her heart to pay attention to what was said by Paul. And when she was baptized along with her household, she earnestly entreated us, saying, 'If in your opinion I am one really convinced (that Jesus is the Messiah and the Author of salvation), and that I will be faithful to the Lord, come to my house and stay.' And she induced us (to do it)." (Acts 16:13, 14, 15, *Amplified New Testament*).

Advantages of Working Outside the Home

Some women find that working outside the home *gives the family special advantages.* Barry and Alma, for example, were concerned because they could not give more to missions. "Here I am," said Alma, "sitting home all day with no children. I could be working to help support a missionary." She and Barry talked it over, then decided they could honor the Lord in this way. She looked around and located a part-time job with an attorney. She was able to give most of her check each month to a missionary and his wife who were going to a foreign field. Later, Alma remarked, "Now I feel I have a real purpose in living. I am doing something to evangelize the world."

In the case of George and Darlene there was a different motive for her working outside the home. They disliked the secular influence in the school. Their son was learning all right, but the learning was off-centered. It left God, the Creator of the universe, out. There was a fine Christian school in town but they couldn't afford to send him. The extra family income enabled them to give him a Christian education. Later, George remarked, "We have seen such an improvement in our boy's behavior since he transferred to the Christian school. We feel it is well worth the investment." Many families find that they can give themselves a boost spiritually if the wife works for a while away from the home.

"Working in an office," said Rachel, "has done much *to teach me how to organize my work.* My efficiency has gone up 200 per cent. I know how to do in an hour what I used to get done in a half a day. Before I went out to work I never seemed to be able to accomplish much. I suppose working in an office has been a school of efficiency for me." It is true that many women have never learned to get things organized until they worked outside the home where they had instruction and supervision. After achieving a measure of efficiency they have learned to apply it to all they do — including their work at home.

"The thing I like about my job," remarked Karen, *"is that I feel needed.* Everyone at the office treats me wonderfully. I like the environment, too. We have a beautiful office and wonderful new furnishings and equipment." Through no fault of their own, some women have to live in homes and neighborhoods that are everything except inspirational. Getting out of their houses and shouldering responsibilities at work is about the only really bright spot in their lives. And with some, it is the only way they will ever be able to get out of such conditions — to work themselves out. They do not care to work outside the home forever, but they know it is imperative to work for a while if they are to better themselves.

As Christians, we often hear the expression, "We are saved to serve." This applies to women as well as to men. Can anyone deny the joy which comes to the heart of a Christian in *service for the King?* Consider the office work that needs to be done in your local church. How about the desperate need for a church visitor? You can reach someone that even your minister cannot touch. Many great ministries could never have developed if it had not been for the dedicated staffs of women (some paid and some volunteer) who leave their homes, at least part time, to help carry on God's work.

Working outside the home *can be a real education.* "I never met anyone but high-pressure, door-to-door salesmen," said one woman who started working in an office. The attitude in most business organizations today is that every employee should understand what he is doing. It is not enough that he merely performs a routine task. He is an intelligent person who deserves to know as much as possible about his company's objectives. This means that employees are learning. Most of them have opportunities to see technical films, to read special materials, to hear lectures, and to take short term courses. Through these means many women are learning on the job.

Some women enjoy working outside the home because *it helps to develop their talents.* Dolores, for example, always liked art. But it wasn't until she took a job in an art studio that she really began to improve. In two years' time she moved from the receptionist's desk to the position of assistant director. She also used her newly-learned skills at church and in her home. She was not only a great blessing to others, but she was happier because she was developing.

A woman who has unusual gifts may feel quite frustrated unless she is using her abilities. Although there may be opportunities in the community to develop these talents, such is not always the case. Working outside the home may be the only source for developing and using the rare gifts which God has given her.

Disadvantages of Working Outside the Home

Most working mothers know that *they do not have enough time to devote to work in the home.* The constant complaint of working women is, "I get home dead tired after working all day and fighting the traffic. If I only didn't have to prepare supper for the family. Then there are the dishes. And the floors need cleaning. The washing has to be done. By the time I get these things finished, I go to bed exhausted. Suddenly I hear the alarm clock telling me that it is time to begin this endless routine all over again."

"What bothers me," said one woman who worked regularly away from her home, "is that I always give my best hours, my best disposition, to someone other than my husband and my children. They always see me at my worst. I go to work feeling fine. By the time I get home, I'm like a dishrag, and I'm afraid I'm as cranky as a witch. If I didn't have to go to work every day, I could be giving my best to the ones I love most." How can children feel relaxed around a mother who is tired and irritable? Children easily sense whether they are loved or rejected. Indeed, the dispositions of parents are much more influential than what they say.

When a woman spends most of her time at the office, she actually has *little time to visit friends and to make new ones.* Sylvia, for example, is a very sociable person. She likes to be around people. But because she works outside the home, she is seldom able to have friends over. "The only time I can entertain," she says, "is in the evenings, but I am usually so tired and have so much to do that I can't possibly squeeze it in." It is not only Sylvia's friends who are missing out, it is Sylvia herself. She could be developing into a much finer person if she had more time to mix with people and to be an inspiration to them. As it is, she scarcely has time to live!

Each morning, a host of Christian women across the country get up by the alarm, down a hurried breakfast, then run to the office. All day they work at a secular job. They repeat this same procedure year after year. But the tragedy is that they continue doing it with only one short life to live, and with an eternity facing them. *They have almost no time for the Lord,* the One who gave His life for them. Starved spiritually, they have little time to read and meditate on the Word, little time for a mature prayer life . . . too busy to lead souls to Christ. In addition, their associates on the job may be a detrimental influence. When these same

women go home to be with the Lord, they will be strangers
to their own Saviour. Then they will wish that they had
spent more time serving Him on earth, more time working
with Christian organizations.

Hidden Persuaders

Working outside the home may be God's appointed
place for some married women. But with many, there are
hidden persuaders at work — unseen factors that keep prod-
ding on the inside of the personality. A woman may not be
aware of these motives which are causing her to leave her
home and to seek employment in the business world.

Finances or Family. Many women who go outside the
home to find employment are actually making a choice between their family and their finances. One or the other
usually suffers. The hidden persuader here is insecurity. One
of the faults of the average Christian is that he gets his eyes
off the Lord and *on* the world. Some women are swept off
their feet by the swift currents of the world. They have
earnings, rather than eternity, in mind.

Despite national and international conditions, you must
realize that God has a plan for this world and He has a plan
for your life. The important thing is not what is being blared
over the radio or shown on television. It is Satan's work, of
course, to dull the hearing of Christian women so that they
only pick up the voices of the world and, consequently, take
their cues from them. Once they are in the world's whirlwind, it is difficult to escape. They are the victims of a
"worldly rat race."

There was never a time when a woman needed more
desperately to stop and think. She needs to consider who is
in charge of the universe, what God's great plan is, what few
short years she has on earth and how she can best devote
her time to serving the Lord Jesus Christ. When she gives
attention to these things, she will be in a better position to
answer many important questions, including how to use
her time. This includes consideration of whether she should

spend more time with her family or whether she should leave them, and bring home a larger pay check.

Because of financial reasons, some wives feel it is necessary to work. "We would never be able to pay all the bills," said a young mother. "I may sacrifice some home life, but I would go out of my mind if we couldn't balance the budget."

To her it all made sense. But little did she realize that she was attempting to compensate for a basic lack of faith in God, and His ability to provide for her needs. Actually, God was more interested in her than she was in herself. If she had surrendered the future to Him, He would not only have met her needs in the *future* — He would have given her contentment in the *present*.

In some families, working outside the home is a necessity, but in others it may be a tragedy. If this is your problem, you need to ask yourself seriously, "Should I leave my home in order to bring in more money, or should we adjust our budget so that I will not have to work outside of the home?" A decision to give less time to the family may seem expedient at present, but later on, as you look back over the years, you may wish that you had decided to trim your budget. There is a place in the home which only a wife or mother can fill. A child doesn't especially need wall-to-wall carpeting and beautiful drapes or a car with the latest lines. But he *does* need his parents. Many women who have made these choices wish now that they could go back and change their vote. Only after it was too late did they see what they and their children missed.

Independence from Husband. Some women work outside of the home in order to be independent of their husbands — a sort of socially-acceptable separation.

"I am in a position now," said one woman, "to tell my husband off. I don't have to ask him anything and I don't have to put up with his nonsense. I am making my own way."

It is easy to understand why some women feel this way, if they have been mistreated by their husbands. However, this kind of financial divorce offers no real solution. A woman who is having this kind of problem needs help from a Christian counselor, both for herself and for her mate. Holding a job over her husband's head is not only bad for her husband, it is not good for *her*. So much love is available to all married couples that they should not take out their resentments on each other in such ways. Instead, they should turn to the Lord in repentance, then turn to each other with a forgiving spirit. Many times this is easier after professional help has been gained.

Professional Status. There are many married women who, if they were honest with themselves, would admit that they are working outside of the home in order to gain professional status. Because they are not deeply spiritual, they have a problem with their ego. They feel that others might respect them more if they had a position in business or industry. Little do they realize, however, that no one has a greater status than the child of God — especially the Christian woman who is queen of her home.

Escapism. For some homemakers, employment may seem to provide a safety valve from the unbearable routine tasks of home. "Working at the office is the only way I can keep my sanity," said one young mother. Such women may actually need to learn better ways of organizing their work and of caring for their children. Often they are suffering physically and are in need of medical attention. But more often a woman who "simply can't stand her children and her house" is a person in need of psychological help. She may be so problem-laden that she could well benefit from a series of counseling sessions. Working outside the home, then, offers no real solution; it is merely a temporary and superficial escape.

Other Men. A Christian man and his wife who were having a serious conflict in their marriage went to see a Christian marriage counselor. The husband readily admitted his part in the problem and took steps to do something about it. But his wife looked at the entire difficulty in a rather cold, matter-of-fact way. She was a competent person who was making a good salary in a large firm. About the fourth session the subject of serving God in the home came up. After a few minutes she looked at the counselor and asked, "Did my husband tell you about the affair?"

"No," the counselor replied. "He only made one comment about the office — that he wished you were spending full time in the home."

After having exposed herself with this question, she felt obliged either to say more or to cover it up. But in an effort to hide it, she actually revealed more and more. Finally she got around to the fact that, although she was supposed to be a Christian leader in the community, she had been with her boss on several dates. In the following sessions she gradually gained more insight into her basic problems. She finally faced the fact that she wanted the attention which the men in the office gave her. Each morning one of them would drop by and invite her out for a cup of coffee. In the afternoon another would invite her out for tea.

She was actually not satisfied with Christ or her own husband.

But her problem was not all spiritual. Without realizing it, she was trying to prove to herself and to the world that she was capable of winning the affection of men. She had been raised in a family in which her father had mistreated her throughout childhood. An uncle had also lived in the family. "He was always criticizing me about something," she said. "I suppose," she continued, "that I have never really gotten over this. Would you say that since I was never able to gain any recognition from my father and uncle, that now I am trying to get it at the office?"

This was a turning point. After a few months she gave up the office job and returned to make a real Christian home for her husband and children.

Many married women have problems similar to this. They are looking for praise and commendation because they feel insecure and inadequate inside. But the attempt to supply this by working outside of the home is never gratifying. The very men who lead such women on are usually laughing behind their backs. Many men make flattering remarks to the women in their office. But they would respect them much more if they were queens in their own home.

Your Influence

To understand God's thinking about womanhood, you will want to consider His initial statement about the first woman on earth: "And the Lord God said, It is not good that the man should be alone; I will make an help meet for him" (Genesis 2:18).

This is a cue to all married women. God felt that woman was filling her greatest role when she was complementing her husband. She was to be *with* him so that he would not be alone. Also, she was to be a *helper*.

Sometimes a married woman does not fully comprehend her influence. Because she may be distracted by the humdrum of everyday living, she may not understand the unique and important contribution she can make to her husband, to her children and to her community.

There are many fine Christian women who have lost sight of their God-given ability and have sold themselves cheap to be a cog in the wheel of some office. Godly men know that they need their wives. This means that man needs his wife in many ways to make both of their lives complete and satisfying.

Even though a woman may not have children, she can make life rich and wonderful for her husband (and herself) even under very modest circumstances, if she remains in the home. As today's secular, industrialized society continues to squeeze every household, Christian women are needed more than ever in the home. Otherwise, the little but important things are neglected. The woman's touch begins to disappear. It is likely to become a house rather than a home. Deep down, a man is gratified to know that his wife has chosen to honor him in the home rather than to honor some commercial organization or some boss at the office. As she cares for the home and devotes herself to studying God's Word, she can be a greater blessing to her husband and children. She is also free to help in projects in the church and to lead other women to Christ. But when she leaves the home and goes to the office, she has little time for devotion to her Lord and little time to be at her best for her husband.

If a Christian woman has children, they present the greatest challenge of all. Sometimes a woman works outside the home because she doesn't really understand the importance of molding the lives of her children. The noise and clutter of little ones seem to hide the fact that there ·is no greater task on earth than working with a boy or girl. All major studies of delinquency show that children who go wrong do so partly because they feel that no one cares for them. When a mother leaves her children and spends her time with other people during the day, she is usually saying by her actions, "I value other people's presence more than I do yours." As a married woman, you can do many things during your lifetime. But there is nothing which you can do that will be more important than developing and maintaining a spiritual home for your husband and children.

Our money may tarnish and our work outside the home may crumble into dust, but the souls of our children will live somewhere forever. Indeed, no work can match the significance of shaping an eternal soul. In his book, *The Art of Loving*, Erich Fromm, in discussing motherly love, states that "it is unconditional affirmation of the child's life and his needs. It is the attitude which instills in the child a love for living which gives him the feeling: 'It is good to be alive, it is good to be a little boy or girl, it is good to be on this earth!' " *Fromm goes on to say that the Promised Land (land being a mother symbol) is described as flowing with milk and honey. "Milk," he says, "is the symbol of the first aspect of love — that of care and affirmation. Honey symbolizes the sweetness of life, the love for it, and the happiness in being alive. Most mothers are capable of giving milk, but only a minority of giving honey. In order to give honey

---

*From *The Art of Loving*, by Erich Fromm, Harper & Row, New York. Used by permission.

a mother must not only be a good mother but a happy person, and this aim is not achieved by many. The effect on the child can hardly be exaggerated. Mother's love of life is as infectious as is her anxiety. Both attitudes have a deep effect on the child's whole personality; indeed, one can distinguish among children and adults those who got only milk and those who got milk *and* honey."

When a woman finds that caring for children is boresome, she should take any steps possible to change her attitude, because the marks that she leaves on her children will bless or burden them for a lifetime. Multitudes of children living today will someday crowd our mental and penal institutions. Adults who are most likely to avoid both are those who have had satisfying childhoods with their mothers and fathers.

The importance of working with children in the home has been emphasized in a poem by the late Mrs. G. Christian Weiss. In the first verses of the poem she speaks of looking back over her life and wondering if the days she stayed at home and cared for her children might not have been barren, wasted years. Then in the last stanza she describes the voice of God saying:

"Some day before the throne you'll stand in glory
And hear from Me these words of comfort clear:
Those years of motherhood, they were not wasted,
For lo, dear one, your children are all here."

CHAPTER FOUR

The Unmarried Woman

Millions of women today go through life without a husband. In America, forty-seven per cent of the babies born are boys, while fifty-three per cent are girls. From these statistics one might conclude that there just aren't enough men to go around.

But that is not all. These figures, impressive as they are, show us only one side of the picture. Because of war casualties, fatal accidents and other deaths among men, thousands more women face a single life each year. In addition, multitudes of other women are losing their husbands as a result of divorce.

What does this add up to? For many women it means heartbreak and loneliness. Others, however, actually prefer not to be married. But whether single by choice or not, the unmarried woman has an important world which demands consideration.

At a little social gathering of Christian friends, the conversation drifted around to Christian girls who do not marry. "Why is it," asked one man, "that many of the really outstanding women are unmarried?"

"What do you mean?" asked one of the ladies.

"Well," he continued, "just look around. Isn't it true that a great many of the women who are making a mark in life are single?"

As the group of people talked it over, they had to concede that many of the women who have enriched the world by their outstanding contributions were unmarried. We know, however, that greatness does not depend upon a person's marital status. Yet it is true that women who are single usually have much freedom to carry out their ambitions. Family responsibilities do not block the continuance of their education, nor stifle their opportunities to rise to the top in the fields of their choice.

When asked by a sociology professor what are the advantages of being single, several girls in the class answered, "None." But the picture does have another side to it. There are a number of advantages in being single. In the first place, the unmarried woman often has much more independence than her married sister. She may choose where she wants to live, and even make a complete change of location if it is to her betterment, whereas the woman who is married must stay wherever her husband is employed. In many cases, the single woman has an adequate bank account which she herself controls. Very often she has the opportunity to develop her abilities and to further her education. Another advantage is that she does not have to cope with a maladjusted husband or disturbed children. But best of all, it is often her privilege to serve in full-time Christian service. Many women who have met the greatest challenge for God were those who were not married. Because they were not restricted by family ties, they were able to accomplish great things for God.

Along with the advantages are the disadvantages.

Yes, there are advantages in being unmarried. But, of course, there are disadvantages, too. "I think the worst thing about being single is the embarrassment that I have to put up with," Elizabeth once told me. "Someone is always bringing up the fact that I'm not married. I've even had people say, 'Oh, you're not married? Well, why aren't you?' They look at me as though there were something wrong with me. Why should a girl have to justify the fact that she is single?"

Sometime later this point came up in a group where I was leading a discussion. An energetic young woman rose to her feet and said, "Well, I'm single, and I'd like to tell you what I say to people when they ask such questions. I just say, 'I have never met a man who is deserving of the great happiness which I would be able to bring him.' That usually puts them in their place."

There are various reasons why many girls do not marry. Some prefer to be single. They may have witnessed the unhappiness of their own parents or other married couples, and so do not wish to get "tangled up in that kind of a mess." Some women do not want to sacrifice career ambitions, while others avoid marriage because they cherish their independence. Still others feel that it is not in God's plan for them. But many single girls are not hesitant to express keen disappointment in their fate. In the correspondence that comes to my office each day, it is not uncommon to find a letter from a girl lamenting the fact that she is not married. But for every such letter, we receive several others from women who are married but wish they weren't.

Why does marriage by-pass many fine girls who would like to get married? Some girls are left out because they live in communities or attend churches where there are actually very few men their age. Others miss marriage because they are shy and retiring. More aggressive girls demand the male attention and carry through until they reach the altar.

Still others do not marry because they are expected to care for parents or other family members. They are not free to venture away from the home base, or to make the necessary move to meet eligible men.

The unmarried girl who does assume responsibility for her parents is sometimes forgotten by her brothers and sisters who marry and raise families of their own. They seem to take her for granted and expect her to shoulder parental responsibility by herself. One unmarried woman described just such a situation in this letter:

"I have been living in the family home for fifteen years, assuming the major responsibility for my parents' care. Naturally, the load isn't easy.

"Two years ago, I injured my arms. Special treatment each night relieves the tensions that build up during the day. My brothers and sisters (all married) keep suggesting that I buy the home place. But I cannot. I want to be released from the responsibilities and pressures that have weighed me down over the years. The family insists that I stay put until the place is sold. It seems no matter what I do or suggest, it isn't the right thing. About the time everything seems calm, something happens or someone isn't satisfied, so it keeps me in an almost constant upheaval. I don't want to complain, but I have become the family slave."

Another reason some girls never marry is that they price themselves out of the range of most men. Always looking for a man who measures up to their unrealistic ideal, they let the years slip by without meeting their "Dream Prince." Idealism is fine, but one can go to the extreme. Some girls forget that they themselves are not perfect. This immature point of view has eliminated many who might otherwise have been happily married. Such a visionary ideal may be suitable at sweet sixteen, but it hardly fits into the thinking of one who is an adult. Nevertheless, some women never erase the image of their youth, and all through life they go on searching for an idol of enchantment who does not exist except in the world of their dreams. The following letter is from a woman who is still under the spell of a girlish romance:

"Everybody has problems, but sometimes a person like myself, who has every appearance of solving her own, has the most complex of them all.

"I am not married at fifty-eight, but I have had chances. Today I find myself 'between romances' more joyous and mentally productive than ever. My good health is a blessing. I am able to impress everyone with my youth.

"Each boy friend I've had has finally given me up with much reluctance. I know the last one was broken-hearted, and I do miss him. But frankly, each one cramped my interests, which are largely artistic.

"I dream of returning to Europe this coming summer to continue my studies. Most of all, I wish to look up a very attractive man whom I met when I was young. I think he would be glad to see me. I cannot forget the intense passion he displayed for me at that time, and my overwhelming delight. I was eighteen and he twenty-four. Therefore, if he lives, I doubt he has forgotten me.

"Friends say I cannot possibly find him, but I am free to search. I am converting everything into cash in order to go. I would even give up all security here in America to remain abroad."

Is this only the act of a dreamer?

It is interesting to observe that though this woman seems to be intelligent and possesses a fair share of ability, at the same time she is amazingly immature. Her unrealistic self-evaluation is evidence of a deep, complex problem. To get to the root of it, she will need to meet with a counselor for several sessions and review the experiences which have led her to where she is now. In the letter, she made repeated attempts to build up her own ego, telling how she has had chances to marry, that she is now between romances, that she is more joyous than ever, that she is mentally productive, that she has been able to impress everyone with her youth, that men have sought her but she has refused their love, and that some were left broken-hearted.

She is holding on tenaciously to a teen-age romantic skirmish which she is evidently wanting to recapture. All of this seems to cloud the fact that her "lover" would now be a mature man in his sixties. Would she even know him if she were to see him now — with a pudgy bay window, sagging muscles and a gray fringe edging his shiny bald pate? He is probably married anyhow — no doubt a grandfather by now. She emphasizes her desperate attitude by saying she would be willing to give up all of her security to pursue this phantom dream. Yet, she is not alone in her quest of fantasy. Although many may not be as extreme as this woman, they too have allowed a youthful idea to shut them off from a mature marriage.

Many girls have side-stepped marriage in their choice to follow a career. Business, medicine, law, science, education, Christian service, arts and other fascinating fields present a tempting challenge for many other capable women.

One of the unpleasant ramifications which confronts those who are single is the feeling of being left out. So often there is no place for them. "It is a couples' world," insists

Lila. "When you are single, you are a fifth wheel. You don't quite fit."

Another problem faces those who are not married. There is little outlet for love and affection. Although this need may be met to some degree when a woman throws her energies into her interests, hobbies or work, the desire for a family — for a husband and for children — is still unfulfilled. The quest for love and a family often presents serious problems for the woman who is unmarried. The following letters bring these conflicts into sharp focus.

Shall I marry a weak Christian?

"I am in love with a man who claims to be a Christian but, among other worldly things, he says he wants to have a drink once in a while.

"Because he has all these failings, and because he isn't as strong a Christian as I've wanted, friends say I should forget him and wait for someone else who is a stronger Christian. But I have waited a long time for love, and I don't want to give him up. Do you think I should try to help him, or just start looking again for someone who's really stronger?"

This girl knows in her heart that it would be wrong to marry this man. Yet she is so anxious to get married that she rationalizes their relationship on the basis of "helping him." However, it is a thousand times better to remain single than to marry a non-Christian or even a weak one. As a single girl she can exercise her freedom, but if she marries a man who walks in the opposite direction or who lags behind, she will not only be tied down, she will be frustrated. If this girl is wise, she will wait. This man may not even be saved. If he has trusted in Christ, he needs time to grow in the Lord and become grounded. She should not consider marrying him until he has proved himself in his Christian life.

Is a wide age difference really important?

Girls who have passed the usual age for marriage are frequently faced with this alternative: stay single, or marry an older man. The following letter shows this typical concern:

"My big worry is the fact that Bill, my boy friend, is quite a bit older than I. He is fifty-six, and I am thirty-two.

"He used to live some distance from me, so we wrote back and forth, but we never did get very well acquainted. After writing almost two years, we stopped. Not long ago he moved near by, so we started dating. We have been seeing each other twice a week for three months. Last night I told him that I would prefer to end our dating. But I haven't been happy about quitting.

"I'm afraid I'm confused. I've been trying to discover God's will, and I'm not sure if my will gets in the way, or which is God's will, or which is mine, or what. We had talked of marriage and I was so happy, but I started worrying.

"Bill's love helped me to feel the love of God as I never had before. I have had difficulty feeling that God loved me. But after Bill came along, I felt that if human love is so wonderful, how great must God's love be. I really feel that Bill has helped me to be a better person, and I know I love him. Bill's answer last night was that he was sorry, and if I changed my mind to let him know.

"There doesn't seem to be so much of a difference in our interests as one might suppose. In fact, I keep forgetting his age. There is a difference in our education, but I don't think that has to be a hindrance. He hasn't been asleep and he has taught himself a lot. And, of course, he is a Christian.

"One of my worries is this: How would his age affect our children if we had any? I wish I could just throw these worries to the winds and marry him! He doesn't commit himself very easily. He does seem to be a bit hesitant about telling me about things like his health and the work he has been doing. He has no occupation as such.

"As I see myself, I have a deep need for love and affection which was not met in my childhood. The question, as I see it, is this: Would Bill meet this need? Would I be as happy as it now appears? Would this marriage make me a better person so that I could be a better witness for God? Or would I continue to worry and just make both of us miserable?

"What do you think?"

This young lady is concerned about many aspects in her consideration. Her admission to being confused sums up the bulk of her problem. The great gap in age between this young woman and her boy friend is only one worry: there are many more. She is wondering if she can trust herself to step out in a marriage venture. She is concerned about Bill's stability as well as his ability to make a living. She raises questions about his personality. She is concerned about raising a family.

This woman will be wise to seek counsel from a pastor or another trusted Christian who can help her clarify and resolve her doubts. True, age differences in adults must be faced realistically. By adding ten, twenty, or thirty years to each of the ages, a woman can soon see what she is faced with as the years pass by. In this case, for example, in fifteen years the wife would be forty-five years old, while her husband would be almost seventy. She must consider that at that time she will be in her prime, while he may even be declining. However, if a couple decides to go ahead with marriage, it is important that they keep mature attitudes toward their difference in age in the ensuing years. It is vitally important for both husband and wife to have honest feelings toward an age difference. A person may marry someone much younger or much older but never resolve the feelings about age difference. As a result, one is always sensitive about it. If, on the other hand, a woman can honestly face these feelings and resolve them before marriage, she will be much happier through the years. This also would apply to many other differences which an unmarried woman may see in a prospective mate.

Another problem which besets some unmarried women is the temptation to give in to immorality. Unhappy married men often find such women easy prey. But the Christian woman must realize that she is a child of God and is accountable to Him. She will not only ruin her life, but she must also pay the price for her sin. The Bible tells us the way of the transgressor is hard. Sin can only lead to heartache and suffering. And when the affair is over she will have gained no real happiness or lasting satisfaction. Yet she must bear the scars of her sin for a lifetime. In the following letter an unwed mother unburdens her heart and tells the story of her tragedy:

"I have a problem which is breaking my heart. I am out of wedlock and expect a baby in two months.

"I feel that the best thing for my child and myself is to allow the baby to be adopted. However, I want the baby placed in a Christian home and I do not know how to go about it. I talked to the adoption agency near here, but since it is not a Christian one, how can I be assured that the home will be truly Christian? Is there a Christian agency or a Christian lawyer I could contact?

"I do not have much money and cannot afford to go to just any lawyer, but I thought perhaps you could tell me of an agency that could help me.

"If I did not have the assurance that God has forgiven me for my sins and has separated them from me 'as far as the East is from the West,' I could never live with myself, and probably I would have attempted to take my own life. However, the Lord has given me peace and I have found great comfort in reading the Word and in listening to our Christian radio station. Now, I want only His will for my life and for my child. Do help me if you can."

This girl has sinned and is suffering the consequences. She does not need any sermon. The deed carries its own punishment. Although her wilfulness has led her into tragedy, God's love is great. In Him she can find complete forgiveness and walk again in newness of life. His Word gives the promise: "If we confess our sins, He is faithful and just to forgive us our sins and to cleanse us from all unrighteousness" (I John 1:9).

One of the greatest assets that an unmarried Christian woman can have is her own personal purity. It is essential to her self-respect and her good mental health. Indeed nothing but regret is gained through immorality.

The Woman Who Once Was Married

Couples who are happily married are likely to overlook the woman who is widowed or divorced. Busy with their own activities and engulfed in their own problems, people scarcely find time to look around and invest themselves in those who once were married but are now alone.

The Divorcee. The divorced woman encounters several special problems. The following heart-rending letter touches upon nearly all the problems which face the woman who is divorced:

"Six years ago my husband fell in love with another woman. In time he told me he had been unfaithful and that I had grounds for divorce. I told him I didn't believe in divorce and pleaded with him not to leave me. I could have forgiven him. We had been married for fifteen years and had three wonderful children. But he ran off, obtained a divorce, left me without money and married the other woman who was six years younger than I.

"I have learned to love the Lord more and lean on Him, but I am human and the six years have been lonely. I am trying to maintain a Christian home and raise the children. But it is hard to do it all alone. He wants to see the children at his own pleasure, even to the disrupting of our family plans. Because I have been sick a lot, I haven't been able to be active in church work.

"I come now to another of my problems. Not long ago I met a man while on a trip. He was divorced from his wife six years ago. She has married again. Now I realize I need to get better acquainted with him and wait, but is it right for me to even consider marriage at all? I feel I have Biblical grounds. I do not want to remarry and feel the rest of my life like I am living in sin. I do want to do the Lord's will and please Him. I desire to live close to Him. I would appreciate any suggestions you might make."

This woman did not want to break up their home, but her husband deliberately left her. As she wrestles with the implications of this tragedy in her mind, she probably wonders, *What was wrong with me that I was not able to hold my husband?* It is only natural that she resents her husband, as well as the other woman. Her world is now a lonely one, but through all her anguish she has learned to lean hard on God.

Another problem giving her concern is that of raising her children without a father. Because she has been ill and overworked, she has been prevented from devoting herself to the Lord's work as much as she would like. Now the possibility of remarriage has become an issue to consider. She is weighing it carefully since she does not want to make a mistake. One heartbreak is enough. The question also looms before her as to whether it is right in the sight of God for her to marry again. *Is there such a thing as a Biblical basis for remarriage?* she wonders.

These are problems that confront many women who are partners in a broken marriage. The solutions are not easy.

If you are divorced, you may be trying to prove to yourself and to the world that you were not wrong; that it was *his* fault. But this is no solution to the problem. If you were part of the marriage, you were partly wrong. At least you were probably wrong in marrying him. It is best to face it and say, "This was a mistake. I know I was part of it." With this realistic attitude you will be able to build a future. One thing is essential: take your past to the Lord and leave it with Him. Confess your faults and your sins. Ask God's forgiveness for anything which might have been displeasing to Him, and then go forward in His forgiveness and strength. Whether your marriage failure was your fault or his, it makes little difference now. That is in the past. When you have asked Christ's forgiveness, you can walk into the future with confidence. There is little place for bitterness and hard feelings. God knows your problem, and He knows what is best for you. He loves you and is more concerned to give you a future filled with happiness than even you are to have it. "Casting the whole of your care — all your anxieties, all your worries, all your concerns, once and for all — on Him; for He cares for you affectionately, and cares about you watchfully" (I Peter 5:27, *Amplified New Testament*).

The Widow. No one knows the loneliness and the aching heart of the woman who has lost her life's companion in death. It would seem enough to bear the suffering of separation without the burden of other concerns. Yet, when a woman's husband passes away, she is faced with adjusting to a completely new way of life. Now she must be the provider, the "father," and make all the decisions alone. "Two thirds of my life is gone," said one lady when the Lord took her husband home. "How will I ever operate the business? I don't know whether to sell the place or not. A hired man doesn't take the interest he should. I feel so lonely, and there's no one to talk to!"

The loneliness a widow feels may have numerous psychological connotations. When these are identified and talked through, the tension of pent-up emotion and grief usually gives way to relief. When a widow can discuss her feelings and her concerns, she can see her path of readjustment more plainly. Such was the case of a woman I met at a Bible conference. I had just finished speaking at the evening service and, as usually is the case, a number of people came to the front to speak to me about various things. Among them was an attractive, older lady, who asked, "May I talk to you alone for just a few minutes?" We moved over to one side of the auditorium and I listened carefully to her problem.

"I am almost ashamed to tell you this, because I'm a Christian and, in fact, a Bible teacher. Furthermore, I have spent a number of years teaching in the public schools and have advised other people. But here's my problem: Since my husband died, nearly two years ago, I have been terribly lonely. I know what the Bible says about loneliness, and I have tried many times to commit this problem to the Lord. He has helped me, of course, and I don't know what I would have done without Him. But still, these times of almost unbearable loneliness come over me and I can't seem to get out from under the awful pressure of it all."

We talked for a few minutes and then arranged to meet the following day to talk through the problem further. I met with her several times to discuss the things that were on her heart. As she unraveled her story, she began to gain insight as to why she felt as she did. She told how she had been raised as an only child in an isolated area in the country. Consequently, she had very few close friends except her own mother and father. At the time of her marriage she and her husband moved to another community. Now she seldom saw her parents. A few years later they both passed away, so her whole life was now wrapped up in her husband. In time they had a son. When he was grown, he married and moved away to another state. So again, she had only her husband, to whom she was very devoted. "In fact," she said, "we loved each other so much that we didn't seem to need anyone else."

Interestingly enough, her Bible-teaching ministry had always been a *teaching* responsibility rather than a *sharing* one. In other words, she had maintained a safe distance from her class, teaching it rather than having a close association with the individual members. This further accentuated her apartness from people.

Now that her husband had gone home to be with the Lord, it meant that she had lost her entire life. There was no one else to whom she could turn — no close relatives, no close friends, only memories of yesterday. She longed to go to heaven so she could be with her husband. Yet even that thought was marred by the knowledge that, according to God's Word, there is no state of marriage there. "That bothers me," she said, "because I would like to have him for my husband in heaven. It would be awful if we knew each other and yet were not married!"

As she unburdened her heart, she began to see her problem from a different perspective. She saw why her loneliness was especially difficult for her. She began to realize that she had actually been threatened by aloneness much of her life, since her husband was her only world of friendship. She saw, too, that her tendency to remain aloof and bear her sorrow alone was a hindrance in overcoming her grief. She had these strong feelings, yet she kept them hidden in the recesses of her heart, not sharing them with anyone. But now, openly expressing her feelings, examining them and seeing their significance, gave her the much-needed relief her heart had been craving. Understanding her feelings resolved much of her tension. She also began to realize that no happiness would be withheld from her in heaven. She accepted the fact that if God does not perpetuate marriage there, He surely must have something for us which will be even more wonderful and satisfying.

There are many widows who, like this dear lady, are

staggering beneath the burden of intense loneliness and despair. What they need is an interested, confidential friend with whom they can talk out their problems. They don't need a lecture; they need an opportunity to uncover the causes for their feelings. When loneliness is understood, part of the weight is lifted. But when it is kept within oneself, it can be devastating.

If you are a widow facing life alone, life need not lie at your feet in shattered pieces. Indeed, with the Lord as your source of strength, you can and you must go on. You owe it to yourself. You owe it to those around you (your children, other family members, and friends), and most of all, you owe it to the Lord. As long as we are on this earth, God wants us to serve Him and live for His glory. Many widows have found greater avenues of service than they had ever experienced before. The Lord may have great things in store for you. Whereas before you depended on your husband and looked to him for leadership (which is right), now that you no longer have him, you must lean all the harder on the Lord. But He will sustain you and will lead you in the pathway of His joy and blessing, if you but commit your way to Him. One Christian lady, for example, lost her husband suddenly through death. But instead of giving up, she called on the Lord to help her reach out to others. Instead of taking the insurance money left by her husband to meet her own comforts, she took additional training, then paid her own way to go to the mission field, where she became a great blessing to many. Now as she looks back she realizes that God enabled her to turn a tragedy into triumph!

My own mother lost her husband when she was in her forties. She was a pioneer woman living on a western ranch. Her life was not an easy one, but she knew Christ as her Saviour and Friend. As she devoted her life to raising her seven children, she depended upon Him for guidance and strength. Through the years her life remained an inspiration to all who knew her. Looking back, I understand the secret of her calm and triumphant spirit. As a boy I often looked into her room and saw her kneeling beside her bed

— talking with her Saviour. *She read her Bible and walked with God.* At the time the Lord called her home, her life was still one of victory. "Christ satisfies," she told us. "He satisfied when I asked Him to save me. He satisfied during my years of marriage. He satisfied when God took your father home. He has satisfied in these later years. And *now* He still satisfies."

You, too, can cast your burden upon the Lord and He *will* sustain you (Psalm 55:22). God understands the needs of the widow. With a heart overflowing with love and compassion, He tenderly watches over you and provides for you. Solomon wrote, "The Lord will destroy the house of the proud, but He will establish the border of the widow" (Proverbs 15:25). Indeed, the word "widow" and its various usages are mentioned eighty-two times throughout the Bible. Is this not significant of God's interest in you? And when He speaks of religion in its purest form, He again provides for the widow's need. "Pure religion and undefiled before God and the Father is this, To visit the fatherless and widows in their affliction, and to keep himself unspotted from the world" (James 1:27).

Single Parents

Some communities have what is called a Solo Parents Club for mothers and fathers who must raise their children alone. These men and women gather together for the purpose of sharing their problems and gaining new insights into the role of the single parent. In their meetings one topic often takes precedence over the others. Solo mothers are asking, "What can I do for my children to compensate for the lack of a father in the home?" These women are anxious to do the best for their sons and daughters even though they must carry the load alone.

Although some children do not appear to miss a father, others feel the loss keenly. It is God's plan for every child to have two parents — a mother and a father. When, for some reason, one parent is removed, the balance is destroyed. Now there is a lack and an emptiness which even very young children will sense. Yet, if you find yourself in the position of a solo mother, do not be discouraged. Many well-adjusted men and women who have made outstanding contributions to society are the products of a one-parent home. Naturally, there are pitfalls to avoid in attempting to compensate for the lack of one parent. Yet, if you are a solo mother, there are numerous ways by which you can help create a wholesome, natural home environment.

Face your situation realistically. Since problems are never solved by denying that they exist, it is useless to attempt to hide or ignore the fact that you are a single parent. Face it squarely, and you will find it easier to arrive at a solution. Being realistic and honest with yourself is one of the first marks of maturity.

Don't blame your troubles on your former husband. This usually brings no solutions. Remember, a child is not especially interested in whether his father was right or wrong. Since a child wants very much to have a father (other children do) he sees him as he would like him to be. The child does not have the same emotional attachments or resentments you may have. What interests the child is the present.

Surrender to Christ daily. God knows and He cares for you. The Lord is your greatest resource, and when your children see you leaning hard on Him, they will begin to do the same.

Don't try to be a man. Some mothers, in order to compensate for the lack of a husband, try to enact the part of both a mother and a father. This is an impossibility. Nor is it necessary. When a woman deserts her own sex, she is no longer effective either as a male or a female. Furthermore, what children want most is an understanding parent.

Spend time with your children. This is one of the best ways to tell your child that you really care for him.

I remember a time when I was giving a psychological test to a little boy. He suddenly looked up and said, "My Daddy loves me."

"Oh, he does? How do you know?"

"Because he likes to play with me."

Most children are like this little boy. They know that mother loves them if she spends time with them. Yet, security is only one of the advantages that come when you spend time with your child. The more you are with him the more you understand him — his strengths and weaknesses, his interests, abilities, fears, and worries — the longings of his heart. Naturally, too, the more time you spend with a child, the more you "rub off" onto him and the greater influence you are in his life.

Keep the lines of communication open. Children need someone to whom they can go and feel absolutely free to talk about *anything.* When you are the only parent to whom your child can go, it is doubly important that you be approachable and understanding. He has no one else to turn to. Guard against habitually arguing with your child or challenging what he says (even though he may be wrong). These are the things that tear down good relationships and build walls of resentment and misunderstanding. As a result, he does not feel free to express himself. Yet, by talking about how he feels, he can relieve himself of pent-up emotions and he will be able to think through his problem.

Emphasize self-reliance. In short, mother, don't smother him! Put your child on his own as much as possible, if only in doing little chores around the home. Childhood is a time of preparation for the responsibilities of adulthood. It is not showing love to stunt a child's self-reliance by shielding him from responsibility. Sometimes a solo mother who is emotionally upset by the loss of her husband will turn her feelings toward the child by smothering him with love and over-protection. This may meet a need in her life, but it only adds to the child's problems, and keeps him from developing into the confident, poised person that he is capable of becoming.

Encourage friendships with other children. Boys and girls take their cues from the people around them, such as parents, teachers and relatives. The older they get, however, the more they are influenced by their friends. Since children need friends in order to feel right about themselves and since they are strongly influenced by those with whom they associate, every effort should be made to put them in touch with other Christian boys and girls their own age.

Arrange male associations for boys. Unmarried women with sons have found many ways to bring their boys into wholesome contacts with men. These associations provide boys with adult male figures which are not available in the home. A man teacher in school or Sunday school is often helpful. Participation in church and community activities which are led by men offer desirable standards for young boys to admire and emulate. Friends, employers and relatives are all additional sources of male associations. Of course, this can be overdone. But some attention to this need is advisable.

Stress salvation and spiritual growth. The most important thing in life is to be saved and to live a dynamic Christian life. This is the ultimate. Since your child's soul will live on forever, either in heaven or hell, it is imperative that you start early to lead him into the ways of the Lord. Then, as soon as he is old enough to comprehend that he is a sinner in need of a Saviour, talk with him about accepting Christ and ask him to make a decision. This can be at an early age.° Follow this commitment with every possible Christian influence so that as he grows to adulthood, he will become a mature man of God. This is his greatest legacy.

Your Resources. One day a week in Pasadena, California, the counselors and administrative staff of the Christian Coun-

°The author's book, *How to Understand and Influence Children,* contains a section on influencing children for Christ.

seling Center meet together for a clinical staff meeting. Much of the time is spent discussing cases and pooling our insights and understandings. Invariably as we reach the conclusion of the case in question, we ask ourselves, "What are his strengths, and what are his resources?" The fact is, no matter how complicated a person's problem may be, he still has resources upon which to draw.

If you are an unmarried woman, ask yourself these same questions. Life offers many problems and, as a woman alone, you undoubtedly face your share. But you also have significant resources. These are many. The following are a few that you dare not overlook:

Your personality. This can either be your fortune or your failure, depending upon what you make of it. And I might add that some of the most radiant personalities are unmarried women. The stereotyped "old maid" personality is a myth. Yet, the woman who lives alone does need to avoid certain personality pitfalls. She has no one to consider but herself. She is independent and is accustomed to doing things her own way in her own time. Because of this, she must guard against becoming "brittle" or "bossy" in her relationship with others.

It always helps to consider the character traits which you admire in others. Are they sincerity, friendliness, vivacity, courtesy, appreciation, optimism, pliability, calmness, humor, confidence, reliability? If you are drawn to others who manifest these qualities, reason tells you that people will appreciate these same characteristics in you. Personality is never static. Although the basic pattern is formed in childhood, your personality is continually influenced by the pressures and conditions of the world surrounding you. In addition, your character is molded by your attitudes and outlook on life.

Your health. There is an old proverb that says, "He who hath good health is young," and no one would quarrel with such a statement. Good health is one of your most valuable resources. It affects many areas of your life, including your appearance, your disposition, and your ambition. Indeed, you cannot afford to neglect your physical well-being.

Your appearance. Not all women can be beautiful, but all can be attractive. Appropriate dress and good grooming are always in style. It pays off in real dividends of happiness, in that a good appearance predisposes people to like you and also gives you inner confidence.

Your knowledge. When you increase your reservoir of knowledge, it not only makes you happier, it also makes you more interesting. A woman who is well-read, who learns all that she possibly can in a variety of fields, is more ready to see the challenges of life. Her alert mind adds to her intrigue and commands the respect and admiration of those about her.

Life would be an empty place without the joys of friendships. Yet, to have friends, one must *be* one. It was Thomas Hughes who said, "Blessed are they who have the gift of making friends, for it is one of God's best gifts. It involves many things, but above all, the power of going out of one's self and appreciating whatever is noble and loving in another."

The world is filled with people who are lonely, but you need not be one of them. As you reach out and show yourself friendly to those about you, not only will you become a blessing to others, but your own spirit will be lifted, too. Do not wait for others to come to you. Many people are timid about making the first step, while they gladly welcome one who extends a friendly hand. It is false pride that makes a woman feel that she has no need for friends. Such thinking only reveals her need for companionship and friends. Friendship is based on two-way communication. Your friends are a blessing to you, and you are a blessing to them.

Your spiritual maturity. God created mankind in His own likeness. This means that human beings were intended to be spiritual beings. No one can be his best when this vital part of his nature is neglected. Yet, because we have turned away from the very *source* of spiritual life — God, our Creator — we are spiritually dead until we come to Him through Jesus, and receive a new, spiritual nature. ". . . old things are passed away; behold, all things are become new" (II Corinthians 5:17b).

After you have accepted Christ as your Saviour, you have basis for spiritual growth. You are born again — *spiritually*. Now, as you feed on God's Word, obey His commandments, and walk and talk with Jesus, your spiritual life will grow richer and deeper. And as you experience this inner growth, the beauty of Jesus will radiate through you and permeate every facet of your life. It is then that you will become a spiritual blessing to all who know you. As a result, your life will be full and others will be drawn to you because Christ controls your life.

CHAPTER FIVE

The Immature Husband

I once heard a woman say, "All men are immature, but some of them are dreadfully so."

I'm sure most men would take exception to this, whether it is true or not. As a matter of fact, the problem of immaturity is a common one, not limited to either sex. None of us is completely mature. Even the Apostle Paul said, "Not as though I had already attained, either were already perfect . . ." (Philippians 3:12).

We like to think that as we grow older we become more mature. But this does not always happen. The steps to maturity lead through certain processes and insights. These may come remarkably early, or late in life, and some people seem to manage to sidestep them completely! So, eighteen or eighty, a husband may be a thoughtful, wise person who is able to see the "big picture" or, he may be immature, much like a child who only sees the closeups.

Ordinarily, a woman's role as a wife and mother brings to her some marks of maturity. Giving birth to a child, consulting medical specialists, caring for and guiding young lives, and adjusting to a mate, all tend to help a woman to leave the land of make-believe and to settle down in the land of reality. But maturity isn't reserved only for women who marry. An unmarried woman may also have the marks of maturity. Remaining single, choosing a vocation, directing one's life alone — these and other experiences also help a woman to walk far down the road to maturity.

Among the many problems that come to my desk each week, many might well be marked, "immature husband." As a wife, you have the privilege of helping your husband to grow and develop, to become mature. That is, unless you prefer to compete with him. But if you do, you are on your own. Your responsibility is to bring out the best in your husband to the glory of God. You can rest assured, too, that you will not be the first wife who has helped her husband to grow up. Every husband, if he is an "honest Injun," will admit that in one way or another his wife has encouraged him to see things more maturely.

No woman gets a ready-made husband. She takes him for better or for worse, with all that this implies, and it is her assignment to make him better, not worse. (Jezebel, for example, did not help Ahab to mature, and this is for sure.)

Women who have taken this challenge sincerely have been a real help to many a man. God has given the wife a tremendous influence with her mate. Helping your husband to become mature does *not* imply that you have a superior attitude, and that you are going to lead him around by the nose, or that you are going to whip him into shape. Far from it. Leading your husband into paths of maturity means that you are becoming more perceptive and understanding, that you are developing more patience and that you are making many opportunities to develop *with* him. You may purposefully pray, "Lord, help me to bring out the best in my husband."

How Some Husbands Reveal Their Immaturities

Every day's mail adds to the list of ways in which some husbands are immature. Many have *personality flaws*. Some men are "picky." They criticize almost everything their wives do. The coffee it too hot, the pancakes are too cold. She is not as well dressed as she should be, or she is overdressed. These men somehow feel the need to keep their wives off balance by constant criticism. They feel insecure in their position and try to buttress it by minimizing their wives.

Other men are peevish. It is easy for them to pout. They grab the newspaper and sulk if they do not get their own way. Some men have short tempers. They blow up easily. In childhood they learned that a loud cry gets attention. Now as grownups they are still using the same technique. It worked when they were toddlers, why not now? By grouching and growling they struggle to maintain their captainship on the poop deck.

"Big-shotism" is a common demonstration of immature husbands. They like to play the role. By giving their wives little money they can be paternal and merciful. They feel the need to be the big man outside, because, in truth, they feel very little inside. All this adds up to an outward manifestation of inward insecurities.

The list of personality immaturities is never ending. Horace, for example, is the "silent type." This is how his wife expressed it:

> "Do you have any suggestion for a wife whose husband gives her the silent treatment? He does it for whatever hits him the wrong way. We have been married 25 years. This silence started within two weeks after our wedding bells had rung. One time he went a month without talking to me. He clams up over very slight matters. He never says he is sorry, and I am always the one to coax him out of his mood. Even so, I have to coax him a long time.
>
> "These moods often leave me ill. If only he would talk!"

Horace is not just the silent type. He is sick, immaturely sick. His pouting and silent treatment peg him at about the seven-year-old level. What he needs, of course, is professional help. A Christian psychologist could give him appropriate tests, then, based upon solid evaluation and diagnosis, help him to see that his emotional development stopped in the primary grades. With proper therapy, Horace could improve considerably. Until then, his wife must somehow try to live and cope with his actions.

One way in which some men signal their immaturity is through their *failure to assume family responsibilities.*

> "My husband and I have been married about two years," said Robin. "Until a year ago I worked, while he attended college. Now we have a baby and my husband has dropped out of school. He is immature and lacks self-discipline. He also tells everything he knows to anyone he sees. Since I have had to go to work part time, we agreed to share work at home,

including child care, but he hasn't done his part. He spends much of his time on the golf course, as if his wife and family did not exist."

To be a father is one of the greatest of human responsibilities. But this role is filled both with potential achievement and with peril. A poor father is a sad sight to behold. Some men have no sense of responsibility for their children. They back away and let their wives carry the load which should be a joint project. This is how one husband dodged his family:

"My husband is a college graduate and is now continuing his work on his master's degree. He is restless, changes schools, thinks of himself as very important, and tells me that he will undoubtedly go to school for the rest of his life. He doesn't seem to find it in his heart to take care of his family. It has been difficult for me and the children. I've worked these six years of our marriage, trying to put him through school. I've even done most of his term papers. We are hoping that he will stop school when he gets his M.A. degree, then settle down and take some responsibility."

Interestingly enough, children pose a real threat to some men. Childish dependence, unpredictability, and discipline outbursts all combine to run immature men out of the home. This is what Bea came to understand about her husband:

"My husband and I had a good marriage for five years until he met someone else. When our children began to come along, he moved in with another woman. He was willing to give up the children, his home and everything so he could be with her. It has gotten to the point where I think he is completely blinded.

"I don't feel a plain marriage counselor would be enough. I need someone who is qualified to understand this 'all-consuming love' he seems to feel for this other woman. It has been about a year since he met her and he asked me to let him work it out. But instead of getting over her like he thought he could, they now can't seem to live without each other."

About a month after Bea told this to a counselor, her husband made a surprise move and came for help, too.

What the counselor found was this: Hal did not like the responsibility of being a father and the head of a family. He didn't know how to cope with children. He had never learned to take responsibility at home as a child, and he was scarcely any better now. Actually, he was not so infatuated with "the other woman" as he was with the fact that she had no children, that she made the decisions, and all Hal had to do was to "rest in her love."

Bea's husband was immature in many ways, but especially in matters concerning his own children. In short, he was a boarder instead of a good example as the head of a home.

Other husbands may show their immaturity in *sexual ways.* They are unable to assume the masculine role for which God intended them. This maladjustment may reveal itself through various symptoms. One husband may be overdemanding, another inconsiderate, and still another inadequate. "My husband lives for only one thing," women often write. "He never thinks of me, only himself. I'm alive only to stimulate him. If I am tired, he does not take it into account. I should be ready at any time to meet *his* needs. Naturally this doesn't give me much satisfaction. He has no control, like a little child."

Other husbands find it difficult, if not impossible, to satisfy the normal desires of their wives. Childish, immature attitudes tie them in knots so that they are unable to love their wives as God has commanded them to do. The following is typical of the complaints many women make about their husbands:

"I have always been an affectionate, warm and outgoing person. I love my husband, but he is so indifferent toward me that I feel sometimes as though my heart would break.

"I have talked this over with our pastor, who then counseled with my husband and used Scripture to try to show that it is not wrong to have sexual relations with his wife. But it hasn't done much good. He tells me it makes him feel guilty and unworthy. He feels guilty when we do have relations and he feels guilty if he refuses me. Now I'm beginning to feel guilty myself for having normal desires. Do you think I am too affectionate in this way?"

There are many husbands who, like the one above, look upon their wives as mother figures. She is to "cook and sew," but the sex relationship is minor indeed.

A man may give the impression of being a quiet, model husband. But underneath this facade is a deep problem. Sarah's husband is this kind of person:

> "My husband is a wonderful man in most ways and I suppose many women would envy me. We are Christians and both teach Sunday school classes. However, instead of spending his evenings visiting with me, he goes out and spends hours alone in the park. He spies on people in cars, observing them and listening to what they say and do. He has done this for years, even before he knew me. He says he likes to see people making love.
>
> "When I ask him why he acts that way, he says that I am not to blame and that he doesn't know why he does."

What Sarah has is a "peeping Tom." His personality development is not normal and his conflicts are undoubtedly revealed in many other ways at home and at work. Although Sarah can help him some by encouraging him to talk about his feelings, she can't do the job of a psychologist or a psychiatrist, and she should gently lead him to the office of one.

Another type of immaturity has to do with *the family budget*. Finances are not only important, they reflect one's basic philosophy and maturity. When you want to know what is important in a man's life, take a look at what he does with his income. If you want to know what a man is like, observe how he handles his money.

It is interesting to note that some men do not want a budget. They want paternalism. They prefer to carry all the money, then parcel out a few dollars to the wife, if her attitude is right. Psychologically, he uses the pocketbook to keep her in line. He may give her very little money to spend as she wishes. He wants an accounting of nearly every dime.

Other men go to just the opposite extreme. They do not want to assume any responsibility for the family income.

They want their wives to keep the books, pay the bills, do the buying and handle everything. They wash their hands of the entire financial job. This is just as bad as the other side. It is not good for the man, and it is not helpful to his wife. Both extremes give clues to a man's inner feelings. They show his immaturity in matters of stewardship. Actually, it matters little who makes out the checks. But it is important that both husband and wife take responsibility for deciding what is paramount in life, what sources of income are open to them, and how their money is to be used.

The biggest of all immaturities is *spiritual immaturity*. If a husband is inadequate here, every phase of his family's life will suffer. Some men are afraid to face themselves and get right with God. Failing to come to grips with their true natures, they reject the idea that they need a Saviour. "I'll run my own life," they say, and in so doing they show how weak they really are.

There are some husbands, though, who do trust in Christ, but they have a hard time getting through the baby stages of Christian growth to real maturity:

"My husband is all tied up with little ideas — mostly his own. Since he has accepted the Lord as his Saviour, he wants to change things that he thinks God wouldn't approve of. That's fine with me, but I think he's trying to rewrite the Bible. First, he took away the television (that was probably a good idea). At Christmas time he definitely said, 'No tree.' He has also threatened to do away with our family encyclopedia set because the part on discipline doesn't match his ideas. Another thing, he won't let our boy join the Boy Scouts at church because he says it's too much like joining the Army.

"To make it worse, he has conflicts about sex matters. The Bible verse about it being 'better not to touch a woman,' has caused him to refrain from natural relations for several months at a time.

"Now don't get me wrong; I would rather see him living for the Lord the way he is now than the way he was before he was saved. But don't you think he's missing out on the joy and freedom in Christ?"

The husband just described needs to grow. The Word of God presents a balanced plan for living. It is only natural that, since this man is a babe in Christ, he may grasp at some teachings and overlook others. But with time, God will undoubtedly lead him into reasonable paths of maturity.

Since Satan belongs to no union, he is not limited to a forty-hour week. He gets in his licks any time and in devious ways. He even influences an immature husband to neglect his Christian responsibilities in the home and to become a church parasite. The following problem is typical:

"My husband is very capable and holds several offices in our church. In fact, he is on *nine* major committees. He spends several nights a week at church, and we always have to stay about an hour after each regular service, waiting for him to transact church business and to greet the people. It matters not if we are tired or hungry; we must wait.

"Usually I sit alone in church because he is on the platform. In twenty years I suppose he has sat with me about a dozen times (and we go to church every week). During this time we have had four children, but I have had to care for them alone.

"I feel badly that we can't have a little time together as a family. But mostly I feel badly because our four children have had little companionship with their father. He spends whole evenings on the phone calling church people, while our children have no one to talk to.

"I know I married him for love and companionship, because he had no money and he's not very handsome. But I feel so alone. When the children had operations I even had to sit at the hospital by myself. I get very blue at times because of the way our life is going. At church my husband is a talker, but he says very little at home. If I mention to him about being so busy in church affairs, he doesn't like it. I have loved every minute of our children's babyhood and childhood days. But I hate to see them go away to college now, leaving me alone with my husband who is a stranger. We rarely go away on vacations because the church needs him all the time.

"I think about this situation and then I wonder, 'Should I feel like this?'

"I have always pitied women whose husbands beat them or drank or ran around, but I've seen lots of unhappiness in nice Christian homes. I think, too, that being completely ignored is in some ways worse than being beaten. When you're mistreated, you're at least noticed. Does it have to be like this? Is this pleasing to God?"

This case is not unusual. Christian counselors have met many men who have learned that the church is an excellent sanctuary for their immaturity. By "carrying the load at church," they excuse themselves for not assuming Christian responsibility at home.

Helping Your Husband to Become More Mature

If you've looked very closely at bookstores lately, you've noticed that many psychologists are busy writing books on communication. The reason for this emphasis is that effective communication leads to maturity, and hence to personal happiness. Talking has many values. Just notice a small child when he is struggling to form his first words. He knows what he wants to say, but he can't get the words out. They're too hard. So he cries and becomes frustrated. But a few months later, when he can express himself, he makes his thinking known and he also has fewer temper outbursts.

Communication does the same thing for adults; it enables them to express their ideas and it prevents them from bottling up their emotions. But it does more. It makes it possible for them to clarify their thoughts and make better judgments. Arguing, on the other hand, causes an immature husband to become defensive.

The thoughtful wife creates an atmosphere in which her husband feels free to say whatever is on his mind. Try to keep from running up a roadblock and arguing, "Now, listen. Why do you bring that up? You know that isn't right!" Instead, you might say, "Is this the way you look at it, Jack?" "Then, this is your feeling, is it, Don?" "Is that the way you feel?" Ask him to tell you more. And you know, of course, that if you give a man a chance to think things through, he'll likely come around to your point of view anyway!

Have you ever helped a group talk a topic through? You know what happens. They talk and talk, bringing up many ideas, some reasonable, some not. They keep talking. Finally, a few mature ideas start coming to the top. In time, nearly all the ideas represent good, clear thinking. The process you used to help them reach mature decisions is the "talking" process. Whether you are encouraging a group or an individual to talk things through, you will see that not all ideas have great value. But they all have a purpose. They serve as refiners to separate the good ideas from the poor ones. If a discussion leader is patient and skillful, he can draw the best out of a group, and through the process the participants will discard earlier, immature ideas and replace them with solid ones.

This process which is often seen in group discussion is also valuable as you talk with your husband. You need neither to challenge nor take at face value all that he says. Remember, he must talk a great deal if he is to do any refining. Many of his ideas won't measure up to the world's great sayings. In fact, some of them may even be way off home base. But if you keep him expressing himself, he will soon think through his ideas and come up with some good ones. This, then, is one way to help your husband to become mature — encourage him to talk things out.

Many wives have used another method of helping their husbands along the road to maturity. That is, *through reading materials.*

You may never have given much thought to the fact that unless men get specialized training they usually know little about establishing a home and raising a family. They have probably not taken such courses and have not done much reading on the subject. Furthermore, many men have been raised in families that represent everything *except* a good example. As one man told me, "The only thing I know about raising kids is this: *do everything opposite to what I saw in my own home when I was growing up.*" And many men would agree.

Some men are quite unprepared for marriage — and just signing a marriage contract and becoming a father doesn't necessarily give a man the needed understanding.

Sometimes marriage actually dulls and twists a person's insights because it may be a miserable, unfortunate experience.

If you can get your husband to read just a chapter, or even a page or two, about family living, it will help. Leave short, interesting booklets around for him. He may pick them up and stretch his insights.

I'll never forget what one woman told me about getting her husband to read some helpful material.

"I ran across a short article which suited my husband to a T. Now the problem was getting him to read it. Finally, I decided to leave the magazine open right beside his favorite chair. Knowing that he might need a little more encouragement, I put his favorite cookies in a dish by the magazine. Sure enough, that evening he sat down, munched on the cookies, and picked up the magazine. He read awhile, then looked up and asked, 'Is that the way you feel about me?'

'What are you talking about?'

'This article.'

'What article?'

'The one about husbands . . . in this magazine.'

'What magazine is that?'

'This one.'

'Let me see. Oh, did you read that article, too?'

'Yes, I read it. Is that the way you feel about me?'

'Why do you ask?'

'Well,' he said, 'when I was a kid, my father . . .'

The old boy had really walked in the net of his homespun psychiatrist! And the floodgates opened! He talked and talked about his childhood. And he began to see the whole picture. New insights came.

'If I do have this attitude,' he said, 'it is because all through the years my Dad . . .'

"That night before we went to bed, he said, 'Honey, let's pray, shall we, and talk to the Lord.' That very night marked a great change in his life. The article he read had furnished him insights into why he felt and acted as he did."

Another method of encouraging your husband to become mature is to lead him into paths of spiritual development. Your husband is created in the image of God; that is, he is made for fellowship with God. His true self is a spiritual self, not a materialistic, or sensuous, or any other kind of self. If he is not right with God, his true self is askew and his conduct and emotions are mixed up. Like the foundation of a house, if it is shaky, the entire house is out of line, it creaks and bends. So it is with your husband. His spirituality is the foundation of his life. If that is shaky, he is off center and hard to live with. In short, he is immature.

Maturity and spirituality go together. You can't have one without the other. That is where you come in. If, as a Christian woman, you want happiness in your home, a mature husband is necessary. So lead him to a closer walk with the Lord.

You can do this by sweetly encouraging attendance at a warm, spiritual church. Geography here means little. Even if you have to drive some distance to get to a church that is spiritual, it is worth the extra expense and inconvenience. A gospel-preaching church is a real help in developing spiritual maturity.

Invite wholesome Christian friends into your home. They will rub off on your husband. Many husbands have come to know Christ and to love Him through Christian friends. True spirituality is contagious. Your husband deserves the right to catch it.

Remember, maturity and love for the Lord are inseparable. By helping your husband to grow close to God you will be helping him to mature and bring happiness into your home.

Occasionally, a husband is immature to the point that *he needs counsel from one who is professionally trained.* Since we are sinners by nature, and we are all living under the curse, it is little wonder that all of us have at least some bugs in our personalities. It is amazing how so many of us get by without the help of a sound professional counselor. This is the last thing we feel we need. Oh, yes, we will conscientiously go to the dentist and doctor for our physical health, but we are deliberately hesitant and wary about seeking help for our emotional and mental health. And, to be frank, we have more trouble here than any other place.

Take the following man, for example. After therapy began it was learned that he was a Christian, but that he had developed a condition which needed professional attention.

"Our home is in such shambles that I don't know what to do. Just my husband and myself are all that are left.

"Our trouble now, I'm ashamed to say, is with us. I don't know what to do. I'm in my forties, I teach Sunday school and my husband is looked up to in the church, but I'm about to give this up because I can't see teaching children and having a mess like this in our home, too.

"In a nutshell, this is what has happened. My husband has gone sex crazy at the age of fifty. He can't even be around a woman or girl without masturbating. He says that he just gets to thinking, and that his mind leads him into this. I want to be a wife to him, but he says, 'You're too old. Other men have younger women, why can't I?'

"He doesn't have any morals at all any more. I'm talking awful plain, Dr. Narramore, but I must, as I don't know what to do."

This man represents a bizarre problem. But there are many people, including believers, whose problems are sufficiently severe to warrant professional psychological services.

There was a day when to talk about getting counsel from a professional in the field of marriage relations or emotional adjustment was a sure sign that we were only two steps from the insane asylum. But this is no longer true. We have become more thoughtful about the matter of our emotions and the tricks the mind plays on us. In fact, the more educated people are, the more alerted they are to specialized services.

Many marriages have wallowed in the mire of misery for years, when a little counseling from a professionally-trained person would have led to valuable insights and adjustments. The following is an example:

"We have a home ruled by drinking. I am a born-again believer and try to live it moment by moment. My husband says he is saved, but I doubt it. Two-thirds of his time away from work is spent drinking. When he comes home tipsy he picks an argument with me.

"Our daughter told me last night her school work was getting bad because of her home. We desperately need help."

Upon receiving the above letter I encouraged the couple to get professional help. They did, and it was soon learned that he was suffering from a brain damage which had occurred some years before. With proper medication and counseling, he dropped his drinking and became a much better father and husband.

Wives must often lead the way by seeking help themselves. Then their mates are willing to accompany them.

Some wives are living with husbands who are in desperate need of professional treatment. Their mental problems have reached such alarming proportions that serious action must be taken. The following letter describes just such an example:

"I don't know what to do. You see, my husband is very abusive to the children and to me. We never know what will make him mad. It has gotten to the point that I fear for the children's lives and also for my own. Many times he has threatened to kill us. He sleeps with a pistol under his pillow.

"I believe that my husband needs psychiatric help. I have pleaded with him to go, but he won't. He has already beaten two of the children until they had to be hospitalized for almost three weeks. I am afraid to leave them to go to work.

"But I am afraid I will be sinning against God if I leave him. Because it is 'until death do you part.' I can't go to tell my own pastor about it because my husband watches me too closely after work. What is there left to do?"

Although it is a difficult step to take, a wife may sometimes have to take drastic measures to help her husband. When a man is deeply disturbed and endangering others, he may have little or no insight into his illness. If so, his wife should consult medical and law enforcement specialists in order to make wise decisions about the family's welfare.

There are many resources available to a wife who has an immature husband. But one of the most effective is her own example of maturity.

The best kind of teaching is example. If you want your husband to become mature, the best place to start is with yourself. *Let him see maturity personified in you.* In some ways a woman has the jump on a man. Because of her role in life she has many responsibilities that help her to become mature. The husband may miss these maturing factors.

By watching a mature wife, a man often begins to look at things more maturely. And sad to say, if he sees an immature wife, he reacts accordingly, and then we have two immature persons. Naturally, that spells nothing but trouble.

Pray that God will make you mature. Let your husband see the answer to that prayer and he will often respond in like manner.

What will be the end result of your offering to your husband an example of maturity? You will not only help him to become more mature, but you will become more thoughtful and happy yourself!

CHAPTER SIX

Married to an Unbeliever

Interesting dramas are likely to take place almost any-where. An unusual one occurred in New York City some years ago. Just before Ruth and I got our marriage license, we went to a doctor's office for the required blood test. Little did we know as we stepped into the medical center that afternoon that we were making our entrance onto the stage of a real live drama. Across the small reception room sat a young couple who were evidently there for the same reason we were. After we nodded and smiled at them, the young man offered us a cigarette.

"No, thank you," I said, "we don't smoke." A minute later the receptionist came in and said, "All right, who wants to be first?" The young man spoke up and said, "Well, I guess I had just as well be." So he went in to see the doctor. After a few moments, the young bride-to-be stepped over to Ruth and me and said, "You're Christians, aren't you?"

"Yes, we are."

"I have an awful problem."

"Yes?"

"I'm a Christian, too, but my boy friend isn't. I shouldn't be marrying him, should I?"

After a brief pause she continued, "I am terribly shook up. I was saved a little over a year ago and I thought that my boy friend would trust in the Lord, too, but he hasn't. I know if I go ahead and marry him I will be disobeying God. But, on the other hand, I do love him, and our mar-riage plans have gone so far now that I can't change them."

At that point the girl broke into pitiful sobs.

As Ruth and I talked to her, we were impressed that

this was certainly *not* the way to begin marriage. This poor girl was taking a big, important step into a lifetime of un-happiness. Within a few days, she, God's child, would be married to an unbeliever. They would be living in two different worlds, going in two different directions.

Perhaps you are the Christian girl who married with full knowledge that your fiancé did not know the Lord. In the rose cloud of young love the counsels of God's Word were overshadowed. The firm and kindly advice of parents and pastor were put aside. You thought all would work out. But it didn't.

You may be the young woman who was deceived. Your future husband appeared to be a Christian. Actually, he was *prospecting* in the young people's group at the church. Your slumbering misgivings awoke *after* you had taken the trip to the altar. In time, he regarded your Lord and your church with indifference, perhaps even hostility. Now at Christmas and Easter he comes to church. Possibly he has found it easier to come to respectable terms. He does not want the Saviour, but enjoys what he thinks is a reasonably comfortable truce by taking out church membership through a bland profession of faith.

Your story, however, may have had a different setting. Perhaps, when you and your husband exchanged your vows, neither of you knew the Lord. You had a rather complete harmony of unconverted tastes and views. Neither of you pretended anything different. Then you alone came to know Christ, in a special meeting or in your neighbor's Bible class.

Your husband seems hurt and alienated when you speak of a wonderful new life in Christ, with old things passed away and all things new. You, in turn, are amazed now at some of your husband's companions, the smell of stale beer and the card games around the home you want to dedicate to God. You are in a hard place, and you know it.

What can you do? How far can you go? How can God help you? Regardless of how your unequal partnership came about, God is interested in you and He wants to save your husband. Many wives have learned that there are numerous avenues of influence which may lead their husbands to Christ.

Develop a spiritual program.

If you are going to help your husband, you must be strong *yourself*. This means developing your own spiritual life. It is not the weak soldier who wins the battle.

The kind of moral fiber you need is not nourished merely by a little Bible verse and a prayer. It calls for complete surrender to Christ — absolute dedication. You need the very presence and power of God Himself. This begins when you confess your sins and die daily to self. Feelings of arrogance or self-pity have no place. God's best is reserved, not for those whose feelings center around themselves, but rather for those who consider themselves nothing for His sake.

You will gather strength and power as you slip away for a prayer rendezvous with your Lord, enjoy the fellowship of other Christians, attend a Bible-believing church where your soul can be fed, listen to Christian radio programs and read Christ-centered books which bring a rich companionship in Christ.

Put God first.

You do have an obligation to your husband, but it does *not* come first. God must occupy first place in your life. This means that there is a line beyond which a Christian wife cannot go in serving her husband and family. *She must not deny her Lord.* If a choice is forced, she must obey God rather than man. Her first loyalty is to Christ, and when her husband's demands are in disharmony with the commandments of God, she is not obligated to obey him.

At this point a sharp question may arise. Your husband may squarely oppose you in your determination to live for Christ. He may leave no loophole that will allow you to acknowledge God or to participate in Christian service.

This was the problem with which Muriel had to contend. A charming young woman, the mother of three lovely children — when Muriel heard the Gospel at a women's Bible class, she accepted Christ and was marvelously saved. Her husband, however, was quite upset by what he termed her "religious fanaticism" and threatened that he would leave her and take the children if she persisted in attending the little gospel church which brought her such joy and comfort.

The night that Muriel had planned to be baptized, her husband actually hid the car keys. Quiet but determined, Muriel borrowed a car, attended church and confessed Christ publicly as she followed the Lord in baptism, a living demonstration of the power of God.

Others never knew what retaliation Muriel's husband exercised against her for her stand that night, but it did not cause her to waver. Despite his bluster and jealousy, which caused him to talk about finding another woman, Muriel remained faithful, maintaining a model home and treating her husband with kindness. She kept her home intact and raised her family for God. Her life was exemplary, manifesting the love of Christ. Because he could point his finger at nothing, this made her husband all the more angry. Yet her sufferings were minor compared to those endured by early queens and princesses who, because of their unwavering Christian faith, were often put to death by an unsympathetic spouse or a conniving prime minister.

In many areas of married life, a Christian wife can graciously bend to the will of her husband. But where it touches her Christian stand, there is no room for compromise. A Christian wife can neither maintain a good testimony nor develop spiritually if she bows to the unregenerate desires of her husband. It is fallacious thinking to believe that if she attends a worldly function with him, he will be willing to go to church with her. This is an insidious trick of Satan. If he can persuade the Christian wife to let down the bars in this subtle way, he has won them both. Soon the wife begins to lose out spiritually, while her husband loses respect for her and the Christianity she represents. An ungodly mate may taunt or put on pressure to make his wife relinquish her testimony, but when she stands firm and remains true to the Lord, her husband can see that his wife's profession means something vital to her. He may resent the fact that she will not bend to his unregenerate whims. Yet, he must admire her consistent life. In the long run, it may be his wife's steadfast Christian testimony that will influence him for Christ.

Utilize each hour.

A wife who really covets her husband for God will trim her life to the goal of utilizing as much time as possible with him. If you are married to an unbeliever, you miss Christian fellowship at home. Although you do need the benefit of Christ-centered activities and congenial Christian friends, there is a danger that your husband will feel left out in the cold. When this happens, he resents Christianity because it has cut him off from his wife. So, if a woman is wise, she will devote a reasonable amount of time to her husband and try to create a pleasant relationship. It may cost you something to tell a friend, "I am going to be home tonight with my husband." But this very loss of your personal freedom may become eternity's great gain.

Florence, who is married to an unbeliever, has found that she cannot attend every activity of her church, though she is regarded as one of the most dedicated and experienced Christian workers. Her husband is a leading professional man in the community and almost compulsive in his antipathy to churches and preachers. He loves his wife and shares his income freely with her. True, she misses out on many Christian "extras," but she may yet be his only bridge to saving faith in God. In a sense, her faith and kindness have sanctified the marriage and home. She wisely shares a part of her life with her husband, never doubting that God one day will possess him, too. "For the unbelieving husband is set apart (separated, withdrawn from heathen contamination and affiliated with the Christian people) by union with his consecrated (set-apart) wife . . ." (I Corinthians 7:14, *Amplified New Testament*).

Your example is important.

Your husband's concept of salvation is largely formulated by what he sees in you. In other words, he judges Christianity by the way you interpret it to him by your life. If he sees a pattern of inconsistency he will not be much impressed by the merits of salvation. The woman with a sharp tongue and uncontrollable temper, or a yen for gossip, may actually be hindering her husband from accepting Christ. Another stumbling block is often found in the wife who keeps an untidy house and is sloppy about her own personal appearance. Sometimes it's pettiness, jealousy or an immature attitude that prevents a husband from coming to the Lord. One Christian woman complained continually because she was not given *all* the solos in the choir. Her unsaved husband refused to go to church because he thought people were discriminating against his wife.

There is nothing that will win your husband to the Lord like love and understanding on your part. When you are kind, patient and encouraging, you manifest the love of Christ in your life. When you are thoughtful of him wherever possible and consider his wishes, he knows that Christ has something to offer.

Not long ago I talked with an outstanding Christian woman whose husband was a highly successful businessman. As I talked with her, I learned that she had been instrumental in leading him to the Lord. She and her husband were very happy even though he was embroiled in the activities of several large corporations and had relatively little time at home. "How do you manage?" I asked.

"Well," she said happily, "I learned something years ago that helped me to hold my husband and also to *lead him to Christ*. When I was first married my mother talked to me very frankly. She pointed out the fact that my husband was a brilliant young man with great ambition. She told me that I would never be able to change these traits but that I could adjust my life to them. She pointed out, for example, that if he were detained at the office and came home late for supper, not to scold him but to do my best to prepare a hot meal when he *did* arrive — and be happy about it. Through the years I have seen the wisdom of my mother's counsel. Because I have been willing to adjust, my husband and I have had a happy marriage. Knowing my husband's temperament, his impossible hours, and his extended trips, other women have occasionally told me they wouldn't put up with him for one minute. But most of the women who have told me this have either lost their husbands, or have not won them to the Lord."

Public criticism doesn't pay.

Your husband will pay much more attention to what you have to say when you appreciate him and offer him a word of praise. Conversely, you should avoid criticism.

Jan was a good example of what *not* to do. When with her Christian friends she always gave her unsaved husband a little dig. This was damaging to herself as well as to her husband. In addition, those who heard it thought less of both of them. Such attitudes revealed her hostility toward her husband. These stinging words also pointed up her own lack of surrender to Christ.

In public, as well as in private, a husband should be honored rather than merely tolerated. It is worse than poor taste to criticize him in the presence of others, even if done in partial jest. Since you are your husband's image of Christianity, the way you make him feel toward you will predispose him to either accept or reject the Gospel.

Men face herculean competition on the job, so don't continue the competition at home. Let him be king at least somewhere. Respond to the little whims and desires he may mention at times. Even the plainest of women may be a queen in the eyes of her husband when she manifests the virtues of love, consideration and kindness.

Do not permit children to come between.

As children enter into a family, they begin to fill various roles. Some have little or no status, others dominate the family. And still others rob either the husband or wife of his or her rightful place.

When a Christian is married to an unbeliever, the two are facing opposing goals. In view of this, it is only natural that there is misunderstanding and disagreement between them; one is indwelt by the Holy Spirit, while the other cannot comprehend things of a spiritual nature. As these differences become more pronounced, it is not unusual to find either the husband or the wife turning to another family member for security and comfort. Often the "scapegoat" is a child. A wife, for example, may turn to her daughter for understanding and reassurance. A father, too, may seek the favor of the son or daughter in order to bolster his feelings. With such an alliance, the husband and wife grow farther and farther apart. As a result, a Christian wife finds it even more difficult to communicate verbally, emotionally, or physically with her husband. But the wife who loves her unsaved husband and wants to lead him to the Lord will be aware of such pitfalls. Rather than allowing a child to widen the gap between her and her husband, she will capitalize on the mutual love of their child to win him to the Lord.

Curiously, Christian teen-agers in a home are sometimes made the innocent barrier between mother and father. That is, if the mother puts the son or daughter in place of the husband. Under the screen of seeking out constant Christian activities with her children she may be dodging the privilege and responsibility of helping her husband. Thus, the spiritual climate that would dispose Dad toward the claims of Christ may never appear in the home.

Next to God, keep your husband first in your life and heart. He will be quick to sense this, and he will respond accordingly. Naturally, a Christian mother should influence her children for Christ. She *should* spend time with them and encourage them to take part in Christian activities. She must also remember her unsaved husband, and not permit her involvement with the children to rob her of time with him.

Intimate companionship is important.

There are many causes of dissension in a home where one is a Christian and the other is not and, because of this, the intimate relationships of marriage are often also marred. Yet, if you are married to an unbeliever, your husband needs the security of your love. Do not neglect him. Do not love him for the reason that an ant cultivates an aphid — a sustaining diet — but because it is your joy and determination to love him sincerely.

Ethel maintained a flurry of church activity, fawning over nearly everyone except her own unsaved husband. She might have left him except for the security of a regular pay check and other side benefits. He, in turn, had reached the point where he was glad to be left alone, since it permitted him a few well-earned hours of peace and quiet with his dog. While quite tolerant of her independent life, he regarded her social chatter as a seething blank, and was wholly unattracted by her missionary methods and connections. The entire situation had built up for years. Originally, he displayed much affection and sexual interest, but Ethel was always cool and uninterested. She refused to get professional counsel. Eventually she began to avoid her husband by burying herself in a multitude of activities.

In time he "gave up." With his loss of interest in his wife came also an indifferent attitude toward religion and the church. Today, while Ethel remains blind to her own responsibility and privilege as an affectionate mate, she cannot understand his disinterest in anything of a Christian nature.

True marriage makes no such provision for coldness. It is your duty and joy to satisfy your husband rather than resist, rebuff and avoid him. Woman was not made for herself but to complete the man. Many women do not know how much this means. A man is usually sexually more aggressive than a woman, and he will not likely look for another if he has a true wife at home.

Improve your communication.

Communication usually opens avenues of expression and inquiry for the unsaved husband. It does not help to argue with him. Rather, ask him to tell what is on his heart. Then, as you open this door to his inner feelings and reactions, speak your heart with humble simplicity, avoiding any hint or attitude of superiority.

Since you are each living in different worlds, he may feel that he has little in common with you. Thus, the ability to communicate is especially important.

At times he may explode from pent-up indignation and resentment. It may indicate his sense of insecurity and a bid for attention or authority. If he makes a rather extravagant statement, you may quietly repeat it and ask him to tell you more. He will no doubt phrase his feelings much more mildly now, and it will give him the chance to get off the hook. In time he will begin to lower the wall he has built around himself and he will become more open to the good news of God's grace.

Bring spiritual influences to bear.

It is your challenge to bring every good influence to bear upon your unsaved husband in the most wise and tactful way.

The guests you bring into your home may offer a spiritual impact. He may listen to the testimony of a guest out of politeness, but at the same time his heart may be touched by the things he has heard.

Harriet's husband accepted Christ in his own home after listening to a pioneer missionary from the Sudan tell of the mighty work of God in the vast hinterland of north Africa. While indifferent to the church, he found it interesting to discuss big game hunting with this man who was a veteran missionary explorer. The man of God wove the glorious claims of redemption into his travel accounts with such skill and winsomeness that conviction and longing settled upon the heart of the host. In time, the husband and the father surrendered his life to Christ and took his proper place as the spiritual head of his home.

The best of Christian literature should be kept in the home, both for an unbelieving husband and any visitors who may be reached by your hospitality. There is something intriguing about the printed page. Christ-centered literature is often an unobtrusive wedge into a person's spiritual interest and understanding. Your husband may not want to give you the satisfaction of displaying any interest in the things of Christ; however, he may pick up a book unnoticed when no one is around, and God may speak to him through this medium.

A large selection of Christian recordings is available at Bible bookstores throughout the nation. In addition, many fine gospel radio programs are being broadcast on both AM and FM transmitters. A Christian home should be vibrant with the finest of Christian music and messages.

There are some effective Christian television programs. This medium of presenting the Gospel of Christ through music and message, panel discussions, counseling sessions, and a variety of other means, is often effective in reaching the hearts of the viewing audience.

Although it may be unsuspected, a husband's spiritual interest sometimes finds a hindrance in the church his wife holds most dear. It might seem totally impossible that you should be called upon to leave a truly Bible-honoring church with the experimental purpose of bringing your husband under the sound of the Gospel. Although he may have prejudices against the church you are now attending, he may be willing to attend somewhere else. Although it is difficult to give up church ties and the fellowship of warm Christian friends, is the price too high to pay if you should find that changing from one faithful church to another equally Bible-centered church will gain the sincere acceptance of Christ by your husband? If he simply will not go with you to your present place of fellowship, there should be little argument that some flexibility as to denomination or church location may be necessary on your part.

However, it would be wrong to leave a Bible-believing

church in preference to one where God's Word is not faithfully preached, even though this may be your husband's choice. Not only will this arrangement prevent him from hearing the Gospel but it may also soothe his conscience into thinking that he does not need to be saved. In addition, your own soul will starve spiritually and eventually you may lose out in your Christian life.

Pray unceasingly.

Pray. Your plea in Jesus' Name is entered into the ledger of God. If He fails you, it will be the first case on record. Delayed answers do not mean a disinterested or a deaf God. A greater weight of glory for the cause of Christ may be in the making. A thousand other prayers may be interwoven in the answer to your prayer. In strange and wonderful ways your own life may be enriched beyond your farthest imagining. Our own motives are so often selfish that we need the touch of God in order to ask anything for His glory.

Don't give up.

Never give up. Men *are* being saved. The fervent prayers of many Christian women for the salvation of their husbands have been and are being answered. Many who had once manifested a seemingly impossible indifference and hostility toward the things of God are now staunch leaders in the cause of making Christ known. God is in the business of miracles. He may save your husband soon.

My mail box overflows with letters from Christian women whose concern is for their unsaved husbands. Yet the picture is not a discouraging one — not when I receive a steady stream of letters starting something like this:

"Dear Dr. Narramore: Just last week my husband found Christ as his personal Saviour! I have been praying for him for years . . ."

So do not despair. Remember that God is "not willing that any should perish." And the next name to be written in the Lamb's Book of Life may be that of the one for whom you have been praying — your husband.

At this time your own personal need is greater than ever before. Do not isolate yourself from the encouragement and help of God's people. Without neglecting your home you will receive much strength from the fellowship of your church and pastor.

The burden you bear can actually become a source of blessing to you in your own spiritual life. It can teach you humility and patience, and lead you to a complete dependence upon God. And because you cannot lean on your husband for spiritual support, you must develop strength in your *own* Christian life. Then, when in time your prayers are answered and your husband *does* accept Christ as his Saviour, you will be strong enough in your Christian walk to encourage him and to help him grow in his new found life.

CHAPTER SEVEN

The Dilemma of Young Mothers

No one knew just how Jeanette felt when Dr. Brownley confirmed her suspicions that she was pregnant again. *Gerry will only be a year old when the new baby arrives,* she thought.

Soon Jeanette will have two children in diapers.

It never seems to occur to Gerald, her husband, what is involved in caring for a baby. He does not comprehend the constant attention demanded every minute of the day. If the baby cries at night, she must be up to silence him, and fast. Gerald says it is hard for *him* to get to sleep again!

As Jeanette leaves the doctor's office she thinks, *It isn't that I don't love children. I do. It is just that I don't feel Gerald really shares and understands my responsibility as a wife and mother. And that is not all. He says he wants five children.*

Just last month, Gerry Jr. crawled out on the front porch and almost fell off onto the pavement. Fortunately Jeanette rushed through the house and grabbed him in the nick of time. But in a few months she will have to be in two places at the same time.

Jeanette shares this kind of problem with many mothers. They feel chained to the house by the insistent demands of child care. No labor union guards the working conditions of a mother, insisting that she put in no more than an eight-hour day or a forty-hour week. She is expected to serve every day and night of the year. Firemen are usually *on duty* only twenty-four hours at a time; then they are *off duty* for the same number of hours. But the mother of small children is on duty twenty-four hours of every day, week in and week out. Sometimes this gets to be too much — her efficiency lags and she builds up resentments against her plight.

Every day, Christian women write our office about their dilemma as young mothers. The following letter is representative of the situation many women encounter:

"My husband and I were listening to your broadcast one day when we heard a case similar to ours. We have been married for five years and have three children. We had our third child before our first was three years old. For about four years my mind has felt like a blank. I can think of nothing but pregnancy, babies, bottles, and diapers. I told one of my friends one day, 'Congratulate me — it's my anniversary!'

" 'Wedding?' she asked.

" 'No,' I replied, 'washing diapers.'

"I work at home from 6:00 a.m. to nearly midnight. My husband does not help. He just sits and watches television. He seems to be drawn into his own little world.

"I am resentful toward my husband as our home needs some work done on it and he just sits and sleeps when he comes home. He was in the hospital this past year, but three specialists examined him and said it was all psychological. *They said he was too disturbed about his family situation.* Can you imagine that? I am the one who feels chained to my house with three little prison guards!"

Another young homemaker tells how her husband takes a day off each week, but refuses to spend it with his family.

"I have a problem and I hope you can help me. My husband and I are both born-again Christians, and he is a leader in our church. We have three children under four. In the last several months, my husband has started taking his day off with other men, going out of town, hunting and what have you. Each time he goes I have a feeling of deep resentment, and perhaps jealousy, because he can just up and leave, while I am tied to the house and the children. It doesn't seem right.

"My husband seems to think I should be content, sweet and happy just to stay at home to cook, wash, iron, change diapers and clean house. Almost every time he leaves, I end up crying, and when he returns it takes a good while for us to get in harmony again. He just grins and waits for me to get over it and tells me I'm acting foolish.

"He has told me to go somewhere by myself or with someone else if I want to, and hire a baby sitter. But I have not been able to discover much that a woman can do without money – of which he gives me none regularly. He has the money budgeted, but seemingly none for extra things except the few things he buys.

"I seldom see people except church friends at services. I want to take time off each week and go with my husband and children somewhere. But he thinks they're too small to do the things he is interested in. I feel so frustrated that I am on the verge of crying half the time. Do you think my feelings are normal and right, or should I, or must I adjust and be happy to go on like this? I would appreciate any suggestions you may have."

It is easy to understand why these young women feel frustrated, upset and resentful. Although it is obvious that their husbands do not shoulder their share of parental responsibility, a closer look at these situations may reveal other facets to be considered. Such problems often stem from warped attitudes on the part of one or both marriage partners. Often, this is the result of a lack of understanding and readiness for marriage. A young husband may feel inadequate or insecure in his role as father, so he "bows out" as far as responsibility is concerned. It's not that simple for the wife. The child is in her charge day and night. And in her youthfulness, she is immature or she does not see the demands of motherhood as a challenge. Rather, they are a ceaseless chore. In other instances, a mother's health may be poor. Naturally, her responsibilities then take on the dimension of a burden.

Marriage often casts a girl into a whirlwind of new and difficult roles for which she is not emotionally prepared. Helen, for example, was a talented young woman with four small pre-schoolers – a boy of four, a girl of three and twin boys a year and one-half old. Prior to her marriage she had been active in Christian work and had traveled, singing in a college girls' trio. The trio practiced their numbers to perfection, had outfits alike, and were well received wherever they went. They met many interesting people and were thrilled to be using their talents for the Lord. Helen loved every minute of it.

Then she met Frank. Some months later they were married. A year after the wedding bells they had their first baby. Others came, and now they have four. Naturally, she no longer sings in the trio. Life is much too complicated. Helen has a rough time even getting to church on Sunday morning. At times everything seems a blur.

The change in roles was hard to take. Helen could not help but compare her present lot with the fun and freedom that had been hers just a few years back. It wasn't that she didn't love Frank or disliked the children. Yet, she secretly felt that they had robbed her of the kind of life she had enjoyed and there were times when she wished she could break out of the house, find her trio friends and appear on the platform again.

Helen blamed Frank for her plight, yet this was hardly fair. He was plugging along, trying to finish his seminary work while he held down two part-time jobs in order to make ends meet. He certainly didn't mean to ignore Helen. But she was certain he did not really understand how trapped she felt.

In addition, she rather envied his freedom. He was on the community bowling team and bowled every Monday night. At least Frank got to drive to the seminary thirty-two miles away. He *could* get out of orbit. But her lot was to stay put, and this was not easy for one who had always been able to go freely.

When Frank came home nights he was up to his ears in study. The children might as well have been in Africa as far as he was concerned. He did not get cross with them — just ignored them. Furthermore, it was Helen's assignment to keep the children quiet so he could study. This almost impossible police task had to be carried on nightly.

By the time the youngsters were all bedded down, Helen was so exhausted that she had only one idea, sleep!

Frank left the whole matter of the children up to her. He seemed to forget that they belonged to both of them, that they both had a part in bringing these little ones into the world. He seldom disciplined or played with them. A smile or a pat on the head, and Frank considered that he had performed his fatherly duty. The rest of the children's care and training were up to their mother.

Helen resented Frank's lack of interest and, as a result, their relationship became strained. In this case, the children were a source of disagreement and misunderstanding. Instead of knitting the family unit together, the children were causing a rift.

There were times when Helen felt that she was stagnating mentally and socially. She had finished only two years of college when they were married. She had so wanted to get her teaching credential, but that was all over now. Go to school? Why, she couldn't even have coffee with her neighbors! She was tired, discouraged and frustrated. She was not enjoying life, and the children got the brunt of it.

Helen's case is not unusual. Many women have similar problems. Young mothers like Jeanette and Helen find that life has become a prison with nothing but "kids chained to their backs." Although they love their children, they feel stifled by the smothering compress of the kiddies' world. They get tired and bored. It tells on their dispositions and, as a result, the whole family suffers.

Since mothers are human, even the best of them with a house full of small children have felt this at times. They love their role of mother and wouldn't exchange places with a queen, yet they feel the need for social contacts with adults. Everyone needs an occasional relief from the pressures of responsibility — a little life now and then; and mothers are no exception.

Can anything be done to help women in such a dilemma, or must they suffer it out?

Indeed, something *can* and should be done. The role of a mother is far too important to neglect. A mother's attitude affects the well-being of her entire family. If she is happy and serene, the children are likely to be well-adjusted and secure. The parental attitudes children sense in their early years form the patterns that will shape their entire lives. This is especially true of the maternal influence, since "mama" is usually the center of a small child's world.

When a mother is tired, discouraged and bored with

her nursemaid responsibilities, the biggest boost that can come her way is not outside help, better equipment or more understanding, desirable as these may be. It is much more basic than that. Help that is to be of lasting value must emanate from within. A re-evaluation of attitudes may change the picture completely. A wholesome, positive outlook is essential to every mother, especially when her children are small. It is the ingredient that changes drudgery into a challenge, and interprets motherhood as one of the most thrilling, most rewarding experiences in a woman's world.

Some Christian women close their eyes to the myriad benefits surrounding their lives. They magnify the irritations and play up their misfortunes. They act as their own "Job's comforters," convincing themselves of their miserable lot. Then they chafe under the illusion that they are the victims of a raw deal. Pessimists? Certainly not optimists! While every intelligent person knows that life is not a bed of roses, neither is it a jungle of thistles. It has been aptly said that while the optimist may be wrong just as many times as the pessimist, the optimist lives a much happier life.

How does all this add up? What does it have to do with a mother's dilemma? Simply this: although a mother's role is one of self-sacrifice and work, it is also one of blessing and satisfaction. When love is a guiding force in a mother's life, she does not view her responsibilities with resentment. Rather, she considers them opportunities to express her love, and she is happy in the joy of serving.

Naturally, there are times when the demands heaped upon her cause her to become weary and tired. That's part of being a mother. A woman's attitude is the interpreter of her experiences. When a mother sees the act of caring for her little ones as a thrilling challenge, rather than as a tiresome chore, life takes on new meaning.

Young mothers, you are not marking time — you are racing it. How rapid the development from diapers to dolls, from bottles to bears, from cribs to cars! Then come the quiet hours of the school day, followed by high school and college. It doesn't take long for baby days to become memories. So, even if you do work hard, it is only for a while, and it is surely worth it. Adjust your sights high and rally to the challenge: *you* are molding human lives.

Missionaries do not stay on foreign fields because life is easy or pleasant. Many times it is difficult, inconvenient, and extremely hard. Theirs is often a lonesome life, with little fellowship with others of like nationality or culture. It is a life of sacrifice and self-denial. But these godly men and women are not deterred by hardships or inconveniences. Indeed, they see the challenge of lost souls in need of a Saviour, and they serve with a heartfelt purpose which carries them through dark and difficult days.

So it is with a mother. Although the demands and sacrifices are not always easy or pleasant, she takes these tasks in stride, motivated by the love in her heart for her children and for her Lord. She does not feel cheated or trapped. She is challenged to lead her little ones to Christ, and to train and teach them to become strong men and women who will love and serve the Saviour.

There are, however, many extraneous factors that can flavor a woman's reaction to her responsibilities as a mother. She may have a difficult time coping with those "little monsters" she has produced. While others label such children as "spoiled brats," the mother rationalizes and excuses the uninhibited behavior of her offspring as the inevitable result of their age or sex. That others of the same age or sex seem fairly well-adjusted is a fact that is ignored. Naturally, having a wild child at large in the home makes for anything but a peaceful, relaxed atmosphere. Mother never knows when she will be rammed by a tricycle, socked in the stomach, or pinched in the leg. This unnerves her, and soon she is screaming at Johnny, and Johnny is yelling back at her. What a relief when night time comes and the little bronco is finally corralled in his bed! Living with such a child is nerve-racking. No wonder some mothers rebel at being penned up with their youngsters. Children such as Johnny offer little satisfaction. Parents do not regard them as friends, but as *fiends* — and the harried mother is "stuck" with them all day.

But children don't need to be incorrigible. In fact, most children are eager to cooperate if they are approached in a positive manner. A mother who is firm, yet friendly, and who combines discipline with love, not only finds that her children respect her, but the home atmosphere is one of happy comradeship. It is during these early years that a basis is formed for mutual understanding and companionship in the years to come.

Discipline is often the key to a mother's release. Although it takes time and patience to train young children, it definitely pays off.° A well-behaved child is a joy to all and presents no drawback in social contacts.

It is also important to encourage youngsters to be self-sufficient. The more Junior can do for himself, the less mother must do. Most children are eager to "help," and even though it may be easier to do a job yourself, it pays to be patient, allowing children the privilege of working along with you. It is then only a matter of time before children can actually help in many ways.

You can eliminate much confusion at home by doing things in an orderly manner and by establishing reasonable regulations. For example, you need not make peanut butter sandwiches all day. You don't have to clean up a mess in the kitchen every few minutes. The children need not stay up late every night. Let them know when and where food will be served; what time is bedtime. See that they understand when and where playing is to be done. Then make sure your children learn to put away their own things. Naturally, you will have to stay with them at first, but before long their cooperation will become a valuable asset.

Time and energy are at a premium for the mother with several young children. A clever woman looks for shortcuts that will lighten her work and stretch the hours. Today there are all kinds of frozen foods, mixes, "iron-on" mending tape, paper products and miracle fabrics. Spare yourself wherever

---

°For a discussion of discipline, see the author's book, *Discipline in the Christian Home.*

possible.* Conserve your strength to meet the rigors of your daily demands and the many extra emergencies that are all part of every mother's day. It may be expedient to cut corners in many·different ways. If you are a perfectionist, you may rebel at the thought of un-ironed sheets or a little dust on the piano. Yet, *you* mean more to your family than an immaculately kept house. A happy, relaxed mother is the greatest asset of family life. If you are a slave to your home, perhaps it is time to free yourself by cutting down on some of your work. Of course, you don't want your house to look like a shambles, but if you can keep things fairly straightened and orderly, other projects may have to slide until your children are older and require less of your precious time. One mother expressed this thought in the following lines of poetry:

What Will My Boys Remember?†

What will my boys remember
  When they've grown old and gray?
The pants knees oft were full of holes?
  Or the trout we caught that day?

Just what will they remember most?
  Two little beds unmade?
Or the fun they had at hide-and-seek
  The days that Mother played?

What matter if my ironing waits
  While I smooth out their troubles
Take time to kiss those briar-scratched hands,
  And start them blowing bubbles?

Will they remember mud-tracked floors
  When they've grown old and gray?
What care they if each room is dusted,
  If I'm too tired to play?
  — Phyllis C. Michael

---

*A copy of the small booklet, *How to Save Time*, is available from the author, Box 206, Pasadena, Calif.

†From *Poems for Mothers*, © 1963 by Phyllis C. Michael, published by Zondervan, Grand Rapids. Used by permission.

Another valuable morale-booster is the ability to laugh. Youngsters seem to have a built-in instinct for getting into trouble, but rather than let your blood pressure soar, try sharpening up your sense of humor. The ability to see the funny side of an otherwise unpleasant situation is a tonic for tense nerves. Try laughing instead of crying when little Susie, in her nice dress, decides to bake mud pies. The reaction of "horrors!" is a very natural one — but you must admit, she does look funny.

Sometimes when a woman rebels against the responsibilities placed upon her as a mother, she is demonstrating her own lack of stability and maturity. She is loathe to relinquish the freedom she enjoyed before the children "interfered." She has never realistically faced the fact that she is now a grown woman with adult responsibilities. She is basically selfish, measuring happiness in terms of what she receives rather than what she can give to others. Surely her children are not to blame for her unhappiness. They are innocent victims of a mother who has never grown up.

To leave it at this would be unfair. You may *not* be selfish, immature, or unstable, but you may still be overwhelmed by the pressures and demands that engulf you as a mother. Harried and exhausted much of the time, you know that your patience has worn thin and that you are often "cranky" with the children. This makes you ashamed, because you really do love them. Yet you seem powerless to change the situation and you feel you are in a rut.

If this is your situation, you may be suffering from a health problem. The physical strain of child bearing, an infection, or a dietary deficiency are often the culprits that keep a mother feeling low and enervated. When a person doesn't feel well, everything is a chore, and little difficulties loom up like mountains. A doctor's prescription, or a jar of vitamin pills, may be just the thing to lift a young mother back to the place of vibrant health and happiness. Trapped? Not now. She's *free* to enjoy her children.

Although a mother is the center of a small child's world, she is *not* the whole sphere. Up to now our discussion of the problem has included only mothers, but we cannot ignore the fact that children have fathers, too. Were we to exempt fathers from their responsibilities in the care and training of their little ones, it would be a gross injustice to all involved. The God-given role of the father is just as important as that of the mother, though different, of course. Unfortunately, modern culture has made it easy for Dad to bow out of the kiddies' realm. This is not always intentional. Sometimes a husband must be educated as to how much of a load Mom is carrying, and as to the part he should shoulder in this partnership. A wife who casts herself as a martyr, suffering in silence, may find her resentment popping out in the form of chronic headaches or a touchy temper. She determines that if her husband can't see how hard she is working or how tired she is, she is not going to tell him.

But this is no solution. It isn't fair to either of you. If your husband doesn't notice that you are bogged down and need his help, speak up. This is much better than pouting, and it may do the trick. You might wait from now until doomsday and he still would never notice that you were in a bind. So, swallow your pride and enlist your husband's cooperation by talking things over with him. He is the father, you know!

It may take time before a husband learns to assume his share of parental responsibility. Many times it is up to you to help him. This does not suggest whining, complaining or nagging. Such methods do more harm than good. He conditions himself to your complaints and closes his ears to what you have to say.

There is a way to get through to him, however. If you understand male psychology, you know that men are gluttons for compliments. They thrive on them and never seem to get enough. If you will capitalize on this characteristic and learn to be generous with compliments, your husband will eventually jump over the moon for you. This applies to child care as well as to other things. Try praising him for his efforts with the children. He may be unperceptive and all thumbs, but encourage him anyway by telling him how well he is doing. True, he probably can't hold a candle to you, but he *can* learn. Many men feel that they are pretty clumsy

with children. So, if you continually correct him and criticize his efforts, he will take it that you don't want his assistance. Since he isn't too keen on the job anyway, he will
figure this is his clue to give up.

In addition to complimenting him, try to involve your
husband with the children. When he comes home, share
with him the things they have done. Tell him of their tricks
and trials throughout the day. Involve him in their feats,
feelings, faults, and falls. In this way you can see to it that
he does not become a stranger to his own children. The joy
of learning about their doings carries with it a concern for
their well-being. As he begins to realize how much is en-
tailed in attending to the needs and activities of the children,
he will begin to understand your exacting task. With this
awareness, the conscientious father will begin to lift some
of the load and allow his wife to get out from under it all
for a breath of fresh air.

When a father really gets involved with the children,
he begins to realize that he is missing something by not
being with them. With all the exciting changes taking place
from day to day, he dare not cut out or he will miss some
new development. And, after all, some day they won't be
kids anymore.

When your husband has an errand to attend, encourage
him to take the children with him. It will be good for all of
you. You spend hours with the children alone, and he needs
to spend time alone with them, too. The house may seem
unbelievably quiet while they're gone, but you can bask in
the quietness and use this golden opportunity to get something accomplished. So when hubby visits a friend, goes to
the service station, or picks up something at the store, tell
him how much the children "love to be with their Daddy,"
and see that he has the pleasure of taking at least one of
the children along. After a while it will become the routine,
so that when he gets in the car he will automatically ask
who would like to go with him. As one clever wife explained,
"In the early years of marriage I coined a phrase which has
done wonders for my husband: *A car, a key and a kid!*"

Some busy mothers have discovered the therapeutic

value of a night off now and then. This change of pace helps to clear the atmosphere and to relieve tension. So, when your husband seems in a good mood, try saying something like this: "Honey, in your work you get one day a week off. Do you think we could work out an arrangement whereby I can get out one night a week? If you could take care of the children one evening, I would have that night free."

Don't expect wonders right away. It may take a little time to get your point across, but if you don't give up, he will eventually catch on. In fact, he may even think the idea was his own. Men are like that, you know!

Several young women in one community got together and worked out a very satisfactory arrangement. They formed a child pool. One day each week they take turns caring for the others' children. On one morning (or afternoon) of each week a mother takes her turn caring for the children of the other mothers. Although this is admittedly a full morning, she still has the one morning free. In this way, each mother knows that her children are in excellent hands while she utilizes this precious free time in any way she wishes. Many arrangements like this can be devised to help a mother.

Some women have found that it relieves them of pressure to have someone come in for an afternoon or a day each week to help with the house cleaning and other projects. They feel that being released from doing the basic washing or cleaning is well worth the expenditure. When June brought up this idea to her husband he immediately voiced his resistance, "It costs too much." But June showed him that by careful planning they could afford it, and that if necessary she would do without something else so that she could have this help. They tried it, and it worked out well. "It isn't just the work accomplished that I appreciate," she said. "It is knowing that at least once a week certain things will be done."

Being a mother is a God-given privilege, and in many ways a much easier one than it was even a few years ago. Our scientific age has rushed in an "era of magic" in modern conveniences. Because today's woman enjoys such specialized equipment as automatic washers, dryers and countless other mechanical devices, much of her work has moved away from the category of hard labor. Too, women are no longer isolated from the world. With television in the living room, a radio in the kitchen and bedroom, and a phone near by, she has immediate contact with others. The door to pleasure and information is hers to open by a mere flick of the switch, while her social contacts flourish with the aid of a mouthpiece and dial. Neither is she cut off from outside activities. Most churches provide nurseries for services and other church functions. This gives mothers an opportunity to participate in church activities and to enjoy the fellowship of other Christians. Nor is the taking of "small fry" the burden it once was. With car beds, car seats, canned baby foods and a host of other baby products, going places with younger members of the family is not nearly the chore it used to be. In fact, as a mother, you've never had it so good!

It always helps to count your blessings and to praise the One from whom all blessings flow. There is so much to be thankful for. Are your little ones blessed with strong limbs and a healthy body? Do they manifest alert minds and winsome personalities? Are you able to supply their physical needs of food, shelter and clothes? If your youngsters enjoy only a portion of these benefits they are privileged. Many children in the world do not enjoy these advantages. It is good, once in a while, *to simply thank God for the privilege of being a mother.* There are countless numbers of women to whom this blessing is denied. And they would give anything for the opportunity of caring for children like yours.

It is true that if you are the mother of small children, you do face certain problems. You may find yourself in the midst of a dilemma, tired and frustrated by the incessant demands of motherhood. Your own physical or emotional health may be such that you need professional help. Yet, if you are a child of God and have committed your way unto Him, you have a resource that cannot fail. God is interested in you — in every detail of your life. With arms outstretched and a voice of loving compassion, Jesus speaks to you, "Come unto me, all ye that labour and are heavy laden, and I will give you rest" (Matthew 11:28).

Truly, " . . . they that wait upon the Lord shall renew their strength; they shall mount up with wings as eagles; they shall run, and not be weary, they shall walk, and not faint" (Isaiah 40:31).

The Mother's Prayer

Lord, give me patience while the little hands
    Engage me with their ceaseless, small demands.
Oh, give me gentle words and smiling eyes
    . And keep my lips from hasty, sharp replies.
Let not weariness, confusion, and noise
    Obscure my vision of life's fleeting joys.
Then, when in years to come my house is still,
    No bitter memories its rooms shall fill.

— *Anonymous*

CHAPTER EIGHT

When Love Is Not There

Wanda was anything but happy.

On the surface things seemed fine. Her husband, Jim, was a successful attorney, they lived in a beautiful home, and had two wonderful children. They were all Christians. Yet something was wrong, very wrong.

When Wanda and Jim were first married, things seemed to go quite smoothly. As time went on, however, a change took place. Although she didn't know just when the change took place, she knew that for some time she had not felt the same toward her husband. She continued as an efficient housekeeper and an understanding mother, but Jim began to sense the change toward him. She was ultra-critical and unresponsive. She seemed to be miles away in her thoughts.

One evening as they were seated in the living room alone, he hesitatingly inquired, "Honey, have I done something to hurt you?"

"Not especially. Why do you ask?"

"Well, it may be my imagination but it seems like you've been cool toward me for the past few months."

There was a deadening silence. Then Wanda replied, "No, I'm afraid it's not your imagination. Frankly, I just don't feel toward you as I used to, Jim. It will probably hurt you to hear me say this, but I — well, I just don't seem to care anymore."

"What do you mean, Wanda?" Jim asked in amazement. "Are you interested in someone else?"

"No . . . no, it isn't anyone else. It's just that I don't feel much love for you any more."

Jim could hardly believe his ears. He and Wanda had been active in the church and had shared many good times together. He felt sick inside and hardly knew what to say. He mumbled something about how much he loved her and how surprised and sick he felt, but it didn't seem to concern her too much. Making an excuse about wanting to get out for a little walk, he left the house and went to a phone booth where he called his minister. The pastor sympathized with Jim and asked him to come to his study the next day.

This was the beginning of a heart-breaking experience for both of them. Unfortunately, it is a heart-break duplicated many, many times. The world terminates a loveless marriage in divorce. But Christian women know this is neither a solution nor is it right in the sight of God. Since they do not condone divorce, there would seem to be no alternative but to endure their plight. The result is misery for all concerned.

What are the dynamics of such a marriage disintegration? What are the causes behind such a problem?

Were you to ask Wanda or another such woman why she thought she no longer loved her husband she could undoubtedly pour out a long list of grievances. Although she is probably sincere in considering these complaints as a basis for the love-lack she feels, she is actually justifying herself by rationalizing. On the surface these may appear to be the causes for the rift in their relationship. But actually, the real reasons usually lie deeply hidden and are not easily discerned.

A rift in a marriage is not always caused by anything either of the marriage partners is doing or has done. Instead, it may be a reflection of what has happened to one or both during childhood. In the exhilaration of romantic love and the exuberance of youth, these subtle influences are often concealed. But after a few years, or even a few months, when the glamor of marriage has changed to grass roots living, the insecurities and frustrations of one's childhood may crop up to mar an otherwise happy marriage. Following are several of the influences which may bring a woman to feel, "I don't love my husband."

The Woman Who Has Not Had a Satisfying Adolescence

Some years ago I saw a film which depicted the needs of childhood. Although most of the scenes have faded with time, one concept clearly stands out and has persistently shaped my thinking. The statement was, "Every child needs a long, satisfying childhood if he is to remain satisfied throughout life." This is true of adolescence as well as childhood. If a person is to be a happy, well-adjusted adult, he needs to go through a number of years of wholesome adolescent experiences. The years between childhood and adulthood have purposes — important ones. They are years of preparation, years that offer experiences that will equip a young person for the responsibilities of adulthood. If the years are cut short or if their purposes are thwarted, a young person must bear a handicap for years.

Here are some of the adjustments and developmental tasks faced by adolescent girls. It is easy to see that the young lady who meets them successfully is much better prepared to meet the demands of love and marriage.

Adjusting to her physical self

Each adolescent girl must accustom herself to the changes taking place in her body. She may not like the fact that she is too tall, too short, too fat, too plain, or too something else. But unless she comes to the place where she recognizes her limitations as well as her strengths, she will go through life unrealistically bolstering her twisted self-images and gnarled attitudes.

Balancing between dependence and independence

Some adolescent girls don't want to grow up, while others can't wait. Some cling to their mother dependence and shy away from responsibility. Others tend to "go wild" when they see their chance to be on their own. But neither extreme is healthy. During these transition years it is vitally important that a girl establish a balance if she is to be at her best as a wife and homemaker in the years to come.

Giving and receiving affection

Contrary to popular opinion, studies show that an affectionate person is not completely so by nature. It is a characteristic that is learned and developed during childhood and adolescence. When it is neglected, or not learned properly, the lack often shows up in adult life. As a result, many wives (and husbands, too) are incapable of giving or receiving love and affection.

Relating to Others

While one emotionally-starved person may withdraw into the protective shell of being a "loner," another will crave and seek companionship to the point of the extreme. Neither is healthy. God intends for life to be balanced. Although childhood sets the pattern for one's social development, the adolescent and teen years crystallize and polish one's ability to get along with others.

Learning her appropriate sex role

The adolescent girl must learn to feel comfortable in her own sex role. She needs to know what is appropriate to the dignity of womanhood. She is challenged to be feminine without using her femininity as a weapon, without being babyish or flirtatious.

Adjusting to or controlling the environment

The countless demands of womanhood make it important to be a pliable, relaxed personality. A woman must learn to adapt to many situations and take them in stride. If this ability is developed during the teen years, it will serve her well throughout life.

Communicating effectively

Probably no one factor contributes to understanding as much as communication. The ability for a woman to express herself readily without anger or sarcasm is an important asset. When adolescent years are filled with frustration and strife, communication is suppressed rather than encouraged. These years, then, should be years of development through learning the skills of communication.

Relating to the world about her

A young girl often lives in a dream castle. She may visualize herself as a great singer or a brilliant author, yet without the makings of either. Facing reality, she finds it necessary to adapt to a routine of life that is quite different from the dramatic scenes of her dreams. Adolescent days allow this girl to touch the ground and consider her actual ability. She can take inventory of her potentials as well as her limitations as she seeks God's will for her life. Without this she may always feel that life has robbed her of fulfilling her dreams.

Developing spirituality

Since people are spiritual beings they have spiritual needs which must be fulfilled if they are to become mature adults. If a girl has never come face to face with her soul's need, if she has never trusted Christ as her personal Saviour, she is woefully lacking throughout life. Studies show that the adolescent years are the years in which most young people seriously consider their relationship to God. If during this time a girl accepts Christ and grows in the Christian faith, she has a special resource which will help her throughout life.

These, then, are some of the developmental tasks of adolescence. But if a girl has not faced and met them adequately as a teenager, she may later, in marriage, interpret her feelings as a lack of love for her husband. Cindy, for example, was very young when she married. Immediately she was thrown into a relentless whirl of keeping house, cooking meals, and working long hours outside the home. Before long a baby came. Her husband was also young and immature — short on adult resourcefulness. Life was now a series of pressures, demands and irritations. Cindy's marriage soon became an endless round of arguments and frustrations.

Although a number of years have passed, and life has become less hectic, something has happened to Cindy's marriage. She *now feels she does not love her husband.* Not really conscious of what has transpired within her, she is now desperately seeking the satisfying adolescent experiences which she was denied: adjusting to her physical self, balancing between dependence and independence, giving and receiving affection, relating to others, learning the appropriate sex role, and adjusting to or controlling the environment. She has never learned to communicate effectively or to relate to the world about her, and surely she has never developed spiritually. As a result she wants to be admired. She would like to have dates, talk about "silly" things, and have a "good time." In short, she has by-passed the years that would have prepared her for marriage.

"I can't help it, I don't love you, and I doubt if I ever did," she shouts at her bewildered husband. He may come back with, "Well, I love you, Cindy," which only makes her feel more guilty. Or he may try to retaliate with, "You don't love me? Then whom are you in love with?"

But the truth is, Cindy is confused. Her trouble is not that she doesn't love her husband. Rather, she *has never had a satisfying adolescence* which would enable her to be an adequate family member. She finds herself in a plight with which she cannot cope. She thinks she is in love with a salesman whom she has recently met. But merely switching husbands is not a solution. Nor can she turn back the calendar and recapture the years which eluded her and left her short on resourcefulness and maturity.

Her solution now has two aspects: (1) come to an understanding of herself and why she feels as she does, and (2) establish a close personal relationship with God, through Christ, in order that she might have the resourcefulness of true Christian love.

The Wife Who Is Clutching Tenaciously to a Childhood Image

"Look," said a thoroughly henpecked and unhappy husband to a friend one day. Then rummaging through his billfold he pulled out a dog-eared photo of a lovely girl. "This is a girl I used to date," he said. "She really wanted to marry me."

Immature men like this can be found on nearly every street corner. But immature, childhood images are not relegated to the male sex only. *Many women have the same problem.* They are comparing their present experiences in marriage with what might have been. Such attitudes are not uncommon with wives who say, "I don't love my husband."

Take Sandy, for example. Unhappy in her marriage, she went to see a marriage counselor about her lack of love for her husband. During the third session a little episode from the past began to emerge. Small as it seemed at first, it gave the counselor (and Sandy) much insight into why she was feeling as she was. The story went something like this:

Sandy was an innocent, insecure girl who came from a broken home. She was barely sixteen that summer when she attended a camp for a week. It didn't take long before she noticed Steve, a tall, handsome lifeguard. He was curly headed and polite. To Sandy he seemed terribly important and rather conceited. They exchanged glances several times during the week and sat together in the dining room twice. On Friday, Sandy's last night at camp, they had a date. Walking back from the tabernacle, Steve asked her to go with him to the boat house where he had to pick up some swimming gear. They took the long way back, through a little patch of woods. Steve, who cloaked his true bashfulness with a bold manner, held her hand. Then they stood for a few moments hand in hand and talked quietly. Suddenly they were drawn strangely to each other. Then Steve kissed her. It was actually Steve's first experience kissing a girl and he was both frightened and thrilled. It was Sandy's first "real" kiss, too. Sandy was almost overwhelmed by the thrill of "first love."

"I'll never forget it," she told the marriage counselor. "I got back to the cabin just after the last bell rang. But I couldn't sleep that night. I kept thinking of Steve. I only saw Steve once more — the next morning as I was leaving camp. But he kindled a fire within me that has never been quenched. For years I looked for someone just like Steve. I turned down lots of boys and never got married until I was nearly thirty."

Sandy's teen-age experience with Steve was so meaningful and traumatic to her, an insecure, bashful girl, that it had left a vivid imprint on her emotions. Now, years later, she complains that her feeling toward her husband was never strong enough to give her the thrill that Steve did. "I wasn't sure I was really in love, even before we were married," Sandy said. "But after a few months, I was almost sure that I had made a mistake. We have been married for five years now and have a little girl, but somehow, I don't feel love for him. He says he loves me, but I can't love him in return."

As their sessions progressed, the marriage counselor led Sandy to deeper insights concerning herself. Looking back with a new perspective, she now understood how her unhappy situation in a broken home and lack of childhood friends had undoubtedly made her experience with Steve assume unreal proportions. She realized, too, that this immature, first-love episode had added to the aura of it all, and that her failure to date other fellows through the years had perpetuated the romantic image which she held.

Of course, every woman has her own set of experiences which may or may not be similar to Sandy's. Yet, many are tenaciously holding on to unrealistic images of the past. They are living in a world of what might have been. They are hopelessly searching for the romantic thrill of an immature, teen-age reaction.

Little do they realize the impact of childhood emotions. They tend to forget the fact that sleek, slender, young lifeguards grow up to be overweight, bald-headed, tired husbands who can't possibly turn back the calendar twenty-five years and reproduce a carefree world of young, immature love, especially when their wives are twenty-five years past sixteen!

The Woman Who Resists the Will of God

When a woman claims that she does not love the man she married, it is often a verbal facade which hides a vastly different problem. The real lack may be a spiritual one. When a woman is in rebellion against God, she cannot hope to enjoy the blessings of a happy, love-filled home.

Take Virginia, for example. She knew better. She was

raised in a godly home and had accepted Christ when she
was a child. Her parents were heartbroken, and her pastor
was saddened; yet she deliberately married a man who
was unsaved. In a sense, Virginia shook her fist in God's
face and said, "I don't care what you say, I am going to
have this man, Christian or no Christian. I am willing to
take the consequences."

So she married him. Soon, however, she began to reap
the bitter end of the bargain. Only a few months had passed
since the day she had stood as a bride, but she was beginning to realize that there was something much worse than
being single. She had shoved aside God's command not to
be unequally yoked with unbelievers. Now she was facing
the consequences.

Yet, Virginia's heart was wilful and stubborn. She still
did not repent and ask God's forgiveness. Nor did she
seek God with a contrite heart so that she would have His
blessing! If she had, her story would have been different.
Instead, she has remained a rebellious, back-slidden, defeated child of God. Her life was in conflict with what she
knew in her heart to be right. Little wonder, then, that she
was irritable and restless. Naturally, this did not make for
a peaceful home atmosphere. Her marriage was a stormy
voyage.

Today, she blames her unhappy marriage on the fact
that "she does not really love her husband." The truth is,
in many ways Virginia and her husband are quite well-
matched. Her unhappiness is basically within herself because, although she *is* a Christian, she is not fully surrendered to the Lord.

Would Virginia's problems be solved if she would yield
her life to God? Many of them would — especially those
stemming from her own inner conflicts. Naturally, she would
still suffer the penalty of disobedience since her husband is
not a Christian. Yet, she would have joy in her heart because she would know that she is right before God and
because He has promised to bear her burden with her. And
if Virginia would pray and live a life of Christian love before

her husband, in all probability he, too, would come to know the Saviour.

Lack of love? Is this what soured Virginia's marriage? Yes. But the lack was not in the direction of her husband. It was toward the Lord. And when she has come back to the Lover of her soul, her heart will overflow with love.

The Woman Who Does Not Understand Her Husband

It is easy to reject and resent people we do not understand. Many marriage problems are actually the result of a lack of mutual understanding. Such couples have never learned to accept each other for what they are. Husbands become impatient with wives, and wives become disgusted with husbands, and love goes out the window. The marriage becomes a miserable existence. Not only do the husband and wife both suffer, but so do their children.

One of the biggest blocks to happiness in marriage is resentments. And when a woman resents things her husband does, she feels she no longer loves him. Many of these resentments are on an unconscious level. They are not understood or clearly defined. Yet their results are the same.

Henry, for example, a college man, is married to Donna who has no college training. He likes classical music, lectures and football games. This she cannot understand. "Long haired" music was never heard in Donna's home nor did her family waste time on "stuffy" lectures. Since neither of her parents cared for athletics, she knows virtually nothing about football. Henry was raised in the city and was accustomed to sophisticated ways, while Donna grew up in a rural environment. Today, even after several years of marriage, she has little appreciation for the things that interest him. These, however, are only a few of their many differences. Donna has allowed Henry's "foolish" interests to irritate her. She thinks lectures are boring, classical music gets on her nerves, and football is a pointless waste of energy. There are heated arguments over their many differences of opinion, and the gap of misunderstanding has widened until it has taken the dimensions of a chasm. Yet, the rifts in their marriage are not beyond repair. If she will make an effort to understand her husband's cultural background and interests, it will bring her a long way toward restored love.

Although misunderstandings take varied courses, Donna's case can be multiplied many times. All too often, lack of love stems from lack of understanding.

Another couple, Dick and Peggy, do not understand each other. Peggy, a Christian girl, was brought up by prim, prudish parents. The word "sex," for example, was never used in her home. Then she got married. *Dick was nice,* she thought to herself when they were going together, but after they got married he was *just too interested in sex.*

The plain truth is that Dick, who has read recommended books on marriage and the family, is trying to be the best husband he can. He is a normal man with normal sex drives and only wants normal physical relationships with his wife. But her attitude toward him makes him feel upset and irritable.

Peggy begins to build up negative feelings toward her husband and finally concludes that she does not love him anymore. But it is not really her fault either. Her attitudes seem right to her. The influence of her parents has rubbed off on her, and, unfortunately, she is unaware of this.

Peggy was really unprepared for marriage. Even today she hasn't the most rudimentary knowledge of the way her husband feels. When she comes to realize that it is normal for men to have aggressive sex drives, and that her husband's actions are according to God's plan for the human male, she will think differently of Dick. If, through counseling, she is brought to see how her childhood environment had warped her attitudes toward sex, she will change appreciably. When she understands how Dick feels and why he acts as he does, her resentment toward him will begin to fade, and when it does, her love will return.

Understanding another is one of the fundamentals (basics) in getting along with him. The more we know about a person, his weaknesses, his strengths, his limitations, his background, the easier it is to *identify with him* and to accept him. Then, instead of blaming him, we are patient, realizing that his behavior is caused, and that his actions are reflections of his experiences in life. When we see the whole picture, we know that he is not directing his actions toward us, and we have no cause for resentment or bitterness. Indeed, it is much easier to love a husband (or a child, or a teacher, or anyone) if we understand him.

Marriage is too important not to work at it. The following letter is written by a woman who is trying to understand why her husband reacts as he does. Even with five children, all under seven years of age, she is making every effort to understand him.

"My husband and I are both Christians and have been married eight years. We love each other very much and get along well, except for one problem. My husband is so jealous of me that he is continually suspicious that I have been unfaithful to him. We have five children, three boys and two girls, including twins, all under seven years. I seldom go any place except to church and to a Bible study class, and then all seven of us go together.

"If a salesman or anyone comes, my husband accuses me of being unfaithful. I never let a salesman in, and I usually avoid talking to men in general. We have had some hard times over this problem, but he has always felt badly after he has said things to me about it. Each time I forgive him, and we pray about it together. I believe the Lord is helping him, as he is really trying to have victory over this. He has told me at times that he knows I have never been unfaithful, but something just makes him say these awful things.

"As a child, his mother babied his younger brother and never treated the two equally. I believe this has partly caused his jealousy today. Do pray for us. God is our strength and our refuge."

A Christian is married for life. If you feel that you do not love your husband, it is possible that you have not made the effort to understand him. If so, there is only one course of action which God will honor and bless. You need not suffer the mental anguish of a loveless marriage. Pray that God will give you love and wisdom. Then walk the "extra mile" to try to understand him. Draw him out. Don't counter him by challenging what he says. Get him to talk about his childhood, his brothers and sisters, his parents, his likes and dislikes, his aspirations and his disappointments. Try to sense *how* he feels and *why* he feels that way. It will work wonders in altering your own attitudes toward him.

Your husband has a right to be a person. When you assumed the marriage vows, it was "for better or for worse." Marriage is sacred, and it is wrong to allow its flame of love to die. A major responsibility in marriage is to accept your mate, idiosyncrasies and all. As Christians, we know that God has accepted you and me, even with all our faults. Indeed, we can do no less with the one who is our life's partner. This is the only attitude God can bless.

The Wife Whose Perspective Is Clouded by Emotional and Mental Disturbances

An otherwise happy marriage can sometimes be threatened by a cloud of emotional illness.

There are many women who cannot devote themselves to their husbands because of their own nervousness and lack of mental well-being. And fine Christian women are not exempt. They have been married for ten or twenty years. Then after a time of turmoil, the husband no longer arouses an affectionate response. She could not care less for him.

When Jean, for example, went to a marriage counselor, she told quite a story about how she no longer loved her husband. "I was pushed into marriage by my folks," Jean complained. "Keith is nice enough, but I simply don't love him anymore. I don't think I ever did. As I look back at it now, I can see how my parents managed the whole thing. The fellow I really wanted was — well, maybe he was a little wild, yet I know I was really in love with him. But my folks refused to have anything to do with him, and they made it miserable for me every time I saw him. Finally, they forced him away and I married Keith."

Jean thought she had it all figured out. However, she did not see the picture clearly. Actually, she was emotionally ill. She was distraught and did not understand why she felt as she did. The trouble began far back in her childhood and now it had caught up with the present. A number of counseling sessions helped Jean to gain an understanding of herself.

Some women experience rather serious emotional upheavals during the menopause. Hidden resentments that have built up over the years may come to the surface. Mistakes and unhappy experiences are magnified while the happy times seem to be nullified. The husband is blamed for everything and especially for her "wasted life."

With "hot flashes," spots before her eyes, jumpiness, restlessness, depression, gaity and general instability, she is not in a good position to appraise her own condition. But paradoxically, she may feel most qualified to do so.

Hence, in this emotional turmoil, she interprets her condition as due to a lack of love for her husband. The worse she is emotionally, the less she sees her own involvement.

While the menopause is a strong factor in some women, there are other emotional conflicts which can bring about similar attitudes. When a wife is emotionally upset it is easy to point her finger of blame toward her husband, when actually, her accusations are reflections of her own condition.

Frequently her attitude will take just the opposite turn. She will insist that although she loves her husband, he does not love her. And regardless of how earnestly he tries to assure her, it is of little avail. She adamantly asserts that he is lying or is mistaken. Otherwise, why would he have treated her as he does?

All this is not easy for the husband to take. To be told that he is not loved, or that he does not love, is very disturbing. Most men cannot take it without responding emotionally themselves. To the husband, his wife is "clear out in left field." How can he respond with love and understanding when she is so irritable and mean?

He might even think, *Well, what can you expect? Her mother is the same way and she gave her husband a bad time, too.* So he barks back and scolds while the tempers get hotter and hotter. The one with the best vocal cords usually comes out the winner. But actually there is no winner. They both lose.

Quite often a divorce will result. But a flight reaction

is not the Lord's way. For the Christian, the problem must be solved within the marriage.

The woman whose marriage is rocking because of emotional problems within herself should seek professional help. First would be a visit to a medical doctor for a complete physical examination. Many times this examination will pinpoint a physical ailment that may be causing the emotional disturbance. If not, the next step would be to consult a competent Christian man in the field of psychology. With this assistance a distraught wife can regain her physical and emotional health, and become a blessing to her husband and family.

The Wife Who Is Carrying Images of Other Men

Psychologically speaking, we usually view people through "previous glasses." We tend to form the picture or opinion of a person on the basis of someone we have formerly known who was somewhat like him. For example, you may meet a person who looks much like someone you have known for years. Without realizing it, you begin to attribute to the new acquaintance the same characteristics you knew so well in your former friend. This is true even though he may be quite different.

We tend to do the same with people who hold certain positions: a boss, a supervisor, a teacher, a parent or some other authority figure. Before we realize it we may build up feelings against a person simply because he is in a position of authority much like another such person we have known. In short, we transfer and attribute to him the feelings we have for someone else.

This is often true of parent figures, because they were so close to us for so long during the years when we were forming our lifetime impressions. It could also be the result of a close association or a significant experience with a teacher, relative, neighbor, boyfriend, or any other person who left a strong (conscious or unconscious) impression upon us.

You may be like countless women who feel that they do not love their husbands. But down deep there are experiences which are prompting these feelings. Unknown to you (or at least unresolved), are dynamics which prevent you from opening your heart and mind to your husband and freely loving him as you might.

A striking example is this woman who wrote:

"My own father didn't want us, so he gave two of us children to the County Welfare. Finally I was taken by a foster family. But my foster parents were an awful mess. They were so confused they couldn't really take care of anybody. I was married at eighteen, I suppose to get away from an unhappy home and background. Needless to say, the marriage didn't last. My husband had an uncontrollable temper and often became violent. I had a baby by him. Many awful things took place before and after this. I lost my baby and tried to stop caring about anything. I became an alcoholic, and during this time had several unfortunate affairs with men. Later I married an Army man. He, too, had been married before and had one child by that marriage. Well, about a year ago I found Christ as my Saviour. This has helped. But here is my big problem today: After several years of marriage to my present husband I realize that I don't love him. He is nice in some ways, but I just don't feel any love. Nothing is there. What can I do?"

The young woman who wrote the above letter never knew the love of Christ until recently. But in many instances the facts are different. Even in Christian homes the real love of Christ and the practical working out of faith in Christ may have been missing. Consequently, the results have been disastrous.

Notice the dynamics which have been in action in the life of the woman who wrote the following:

"I pray you will be able to help me. I have tried talking to our minister, wondering whether I need some professional help, but he said, 'No,' and that's all the further I got with him.

"I am very thankful to have been saved in my childhood. But I was brought up in an overly-strict, unhappy home. In fact, it was not until I reached adulthood that I realized my parents loved me. Then I guess it was too late. I don't remember laughter, playing or any satisfying discussions with my parents. It was all hard work, both physical and *spiritual*. We were always *striving* to please God; never, never resting in Him. As I look back I can't think of one dishonest deed I did against my parents. There were twelve of us including our parents, and we were made to behave. But no love.

"I was always afraid of my Dad. I still am. I can hardly talk to him. He is old now and softened somewhat.

"Now this is my problem: I married a man whom I had only known three weeks. At the time he seemed like the most kind and understanding person I ever knew. We have been married several years now and have three wonderful, healthy children. *But I seem unable to love my husband.* He apparently loves me very much and tells me what a good person I am. I guess this makes me feel guilty. All this time I have kept these feelings to myself. Not even our relatives know how I feel. I am ashamed *not* to love him anymore, yet I can't muster up something that's not there. Can anything be done for me?"

Even though one of these women was raised in a Christian home, the results were scarcely any better than in the case of the other woman who had virtually no Christian influence. Since there was little or no love and understanding, the results were essentially the same.

Both of these women later had professional help from a Christian psychologist. After initial interviews and psychological testing, each had a series of counseling sessions. This resulted in depth of understanding and release. They came to realize that their problem was not that they did not love their husbands, but rather, that they were attributing to their husbands the images which they held of their fathers, foster-father, previous husband, as well as other men with whom they had negative experiences. With this understanding and detailed discussion the impulses began to lose their power so that they felt differently about their husbands. Too, as they committed themselves to the Lord and asked daily for God's love to fill their lives, they were able to respond to their husbands.

The Woman Who Is Not Yielded to Christ

Ultimately the problem of a woman who claims to have lost her love for her husband is usually spiritual. There is no middle ground here. It is certainly no spiritual accomplishment to be able to say, "I no longer love my husband." This is not victory; it is defeat.

A Christian marriage is for life. Most often a wife's trouble comes when she is not yielded to Christ. Because if she is not yielded to Christ, she is yielded to something else. That "something else" is the world. There is a "philosophy of this world." And that philosophy is not of the Lord.

The philosophy of "this world" is that if you do not love your husband, get rid of him, dress up and go out after another. Maybe you'll do better next time. But the end is a dead end street. The joy goes out of the woman's life and tragedy comes in. Distorted children then, are the result of divided homes.

A woman who is yielded to Christ has satisfaction inside. For her, Christ is everything. Her husband comes next to Christ and a Christian husband is happy to be second to the Lord. He could not be more secure than in that position. A Christian woman, rejoicing in the Lord and happy in His service, has the kind of security and peace which makes her mature. A mature woman loves her husband, even if he is immature.

In writing to the Romans, Paul advises not to let the world squeeze you into its mold. The pressure is always on by the world. It gets to Christian women and they adopt the solution of the world. But separation and divorce seldom settle problems. They only prove one thing — immaturity on the part of those involved. For when they are divorced they will have to take themselves along.

The woman who says, "I no longer love my husband," has to answer the question "why?" So often such a question brings a swarm of complaints. "He is mean to me"; "he isn't a gentleman"; "he scolded me in public"; "he is lazy"; "he always forgot my birthday." And so on with endless complaints. But basically it is self-centeredness. "He hurt my ego." A real Christian, however, is crucified with Christ and is not easily hurt, because he is dead to self.

For a Christian woman to catalog her husband's faults and say, "That is why I no longer love him," is a manifest way of saying, "I am not very spiritual and that is why these things are so important to me. Not what the Lord thinks, but what I think."

How refreshing it is to remember the loyalty of First Mate Bob's wife on the West Coast. Prior to his conversion, First Mate Bob, a popular evangelical broadcaster, left his wife and children for a number of years without any means of support or concern. But his Christian wife did not whine or fret; she just prayed. Bob was saved and God has blessed his family abundantly because of the yielded life of his wife.

Whenever a Christian woman says, "I no longer love my husband," there is often pride involved. The presupposition is that she has been very righteous and adequate, while her husband has failed to measure up. In substance, she is self-righteous. In the light of God's perfection, she should throw herself on her face before God and cry out, "God be merciful to me a sinner."

A real Christian love "never runs dry." A Christian woman who truly loves her husband will love him to the end. A Christian woman who is yielded to Christ is a channel of His love and certainly His love never runs dry. It never fails!

There are many reasons why a woman may feel that she doesn't love her husband, but underneath these feelings are dynamics which are often hidden.

Following is a letter from a woman who did not love her husband. It is a rare example of a wife who gained self-understanding, then surrendered to God:

"You often speak of persons who marry in haste, or without love. When you do, you usually warn the youth against this mistake.

"But this does not offer much help to the persons already married without love. I married to get away from home; yet today, twenty-three years later, I have a happy marriage and home. I'd like to share my solution with you.

"In the beginning it was pretty bad. My husband's actions in every crisis and in everyday living were inconsiderate . . . or at least I thought so until I took stock of myself. How is an unloved person supposed to react? I gave a lot of thought to this word 'love' as used in the Bible. Can God expect us to love one another if it is not in our power to do so, or if He will not enable us?

"One day I was saved and I began to know what God could do for me. Was love something that you felt, something that happened to you, or an act of the will? I finally faced the fact that I might not be able to *feel* love, but why could I not *show forth* love? From that minute on I began to behave as if *I did feel love!* What would I do for my husband today, I asked myself, if I really *were* in love with him? Then I proceeded to do these little kindnesses. I studied his likes and dislikes and bought little treats for his lunch box. I tried to comfort him when he came home from work tired or harrassed by a heavy schedule. I met him at the door with a smile. I respected his discipline of the children and worked with him. I tried to speak softly and diplomatically when we had differences. I listened to him.

"Soon I noticed a marked change in him. He was behaving as though he were living with someone who loved him! And I began to notice a change in my own feelings. He was not at all like I had concluded. He had real depth! And I was beginning to fall in love with him!

"Is this why God admonishes us all to show forth love? He has not said to show forth love if you *feel* love, has He? At the time it seemed to me that Christians did all the giving and none of the getting. But, when God told my heart to show forth love, it was really I who was blessed at the end.

"Only last week my teen-age son said, 'All of my friends say that I have it good.'

" 'Why?' I asked.

" 'Because you and Dad really like each other,' he said. 'You'd be surprised how many of the kids' parents don't get along too hot.'

"So, my answer to the people who are stuck in a marriage that is loveless, is to 'show forth love.' "

Sincerely,

A Happy Christian wife and mother.

CHAPTER NINE

The Maladjusted Child

"I don't know what the trouble is," confessed the fifth grade teacher to the school psychologist, "but I do know *something* is wrong. None of the other children in the family have any problems as far as I know. I had Johnny's older brother and sister and they were two of the best students I've ever had."

Teachers echo this complaint in classrooms all over the land. But school personnel are not the only ones who wonder "what the trouble is." Parents, too, are concerned. "Our other children have no serious difficulties," they confide, "but Johnny has enough problems for several children."

A child like Johnny brings much heartache and confusion to an entire family. It only takes one disturbed child to throw a family into disharmony. Many households would be fairly serene if it were not for one youngster who has glaring problems. The symptoms are noticed by nearly everyone, but the causes are usually hidden. Finding the solution is a difficult task. This is the very theme of the following letter. It is an example of what many parents face. The mother is concerned about her daughter's behavior, but she has no idea what may be causing it.

"We have a child who has an uncontrollable temper — she goes into a near rage over every little difficulty, or flies off at any resistance she meets. She will hit anyone, particularly her brother for no reason at all and when she gets angry, she does almost anything out of desperation.

"She has always been an extremely active child. She is big for her age and always has been. I know she needs a lot of

149

love and attention, which we find hard to give her because she's so uncooperative. Discipline is a big problem. Sometimes she sobs until she can hardly get her breath. She can't stop until cuddled or shown special attention.

"I am concerned over the possibility of this problem developing into an even greater one, and believe me, it's bad enough now. If only I knew what was causing her to act this way. I am at a loss as to what to do."

The problem this mother faces is not an uncommon one. Yet, it is an indication that something is definitely wrong. In the first place, a child who has a problem needs help for his own sake alone. He does not enjoy being out of step in life. His is a continual conflict. What is more, if the child is not helped soon, his problem will increase and he will grow into adulthood unhappy and unstable. In addition, a problem child may cause rifts and misunderstandings between parents. Each may blame the other for handling the youngster improperly, when actually, the problem is basically within the child, and not in his parental training.

Developmental Problems

God tells us that we are "fearfully and wonderfully made." One of the miracles within the miracle of life is that of growth and maturation. The development of the human body and personality is orderly. Infants and children all go through the same growth processes and developmental stages. However, because of individual differences, they go through these stages at different rates and at different times. Some mothers become overly-concerned about their child's rate of development. They are extremely anxious that their little darlings present a "star performance" to relatives, and especially to friends who also have young children. So, in order for him to compare favorably, the mother shoves him on ahead when in reality he may need to linger a little longer at that particular developmental stage, before he is ready to tackle the next. A young mother, especially one with a first or second child, is more likely to be over-concerned that her child develop quickly and stay ahead of others his age. The following letter is from a mother who fits into this category.

Although she is a Christian, she is extremely impatient and finds it difficult to relax and wait for her boy to develop at his own individual rate. By her over-anxiety she is missing out because she is not enjoying her child for what he is, and her son is missing out because he lacks the security he needs so desperately.

"We are a Christian family, and our problem is with our boy, aged five. He doesn't seem to be interested in keeping up with other children his age. He went to Sunday school for over two years before he could sing as well as the other children. My husband and I have sung in the choir since we were teen-agers, so naturally we would expect our son to do at least as well as other children.

"It seems he doesn't want to learn anything when you first try to teach him, or if it is something he *has* to learn. For example: I tried to teach him to write his name, and it was impossible for him to learn, so I decided to just leave him alone. One day, about a month later, he said, 'Look, mommy, I wrote my name.' He didn't even have anything to copy it from, so you see he is bright enough. He is the same way about learning his memory work. The other children at Sunday school will stand right up and say their verse, but not he.

"Lately, he has been wetting the bed at night. I know all this has something to do with his nerves and I am concerned very much about his starting to school next fall. We have tried so many ways to get him out of this. He certainly is old enough to have better control. I tell him, 'What would your friends think if they knew that you wet the bed? None of *them* do that.'

"We don't want him to become spoiled or too coddled. He needs to be on his own more. His cousin, who lives near us, is way ahead of him in most things and since they play together, it makes it bad for our boy.

"Another reason why I am concerned about him is that it is very hard to deal with him spiritually because he is so withdrawn and shut up inside about his feelings. I so wish he would talk to me more about spiritual things. Many children at five have already accepted Christ as their Saviour in a children's class that I help out in. However, my boy has never raised his hand.

"I get so impatient. I wish he would hurry and get over some of his baby ways."

Here we have a picture of a mother standing in back of her child with a goad, urging him to move faster. Later on, she will probably wish she had just relaxed and permitted him to move along at his own rate. Learning to walk, talk, play easily with other children, and to care for toilet needs — these and a hundred other developmental tasks must unfold as a child is ready. Parents with several children know that each is different and, while one may learn to do something very early, another may learn quite late. Each takes his own path to maturity, and rushing will not help. He will not be able to assimilate more than his maturation will allow. Pushing a child beyond his level of ability only makes him confused and upset. He begins to feel that he is not successful, and he soon senses that he is unable to suit his parents. How much better to permit a child to follow his own developmental pattern!

Intellectual Problems

One day as I answered the insistent ring of the phone, a woman's voice asked, "How young can you test a child's intelligence?"

"Quite young," I replied.

"I have a two-year-old boy who is a real problem," she went on. "My main concern at present is that he is so stubborn and does not mind as well as I wish he would. It isn't that we haven't tried to treat him right, with the Lord's guidance, of course, but he is just like a mule! It doesn't do a bit of good to spank him. Sitting him in a chair or putting him in his room doesn't work, either. He only disobeys again and he won't stay where I tell him. So, I have to spank him anyway. I don't think it does any good to talk to him or love him, for that matter. Do you think there could be anything wrong with his mind?"

I assured her that much of the behavior she described was normal for his age, and that he was probably passing through the "negative twos." At this state he has just learned he can assert himself, and he does so by saying "no" to nearly everything. "Give him a chance to outgrow his negativism," I suggested. I went on to explain that if his problem continued over a longer period of time, it would be wise to bring him to the Counseling Center where we could help find the causes of his behavior.

Although this mother may appear a little over-anxious about her boy, her fears may be well grounded. Therefore, if the problem persists, she would be wise to follow through with professional help.

Although we can ascertain a child's intellectual development at an early age, we are able to get a much more accurate estimate when he is of school age or older.

Many women are concerned about the intellectual development of their children. The practice in schools of giving intelligence tests to the entire school population, and the many articles appearing in popular magazines, have alerted parents to the fact that their children may be gifted or even somewhat retarded without the parents actually realizing it. Since intelligence has a definite influence over behavior, it is important that parents have a basic understanding of their children's intellect.

One mother, concerned about her girl's intellectual development wrote me the following letter:

"We have a girl who is now ten years old and in the fourth grade, and we are having problems with her. She is so forward, cannot seem to make friends, has lied on numerous occasions and has difficulty in school.

"During the past six months, we have come to the conclusion that we need professional help for her. We are born-again believers, and have felt hesitant about seeking out such help, until a friend told us about your Christian approach in psychology."

I wrote this mother, suggesting that she and her husband contact a Christian psychologist in their community who would be able to give intelligence tests to their child. They did so, and learned that the girl was a little below average in mental capacity. The psychologist explained that the girl came under the classification of "dull-normal." "She can live a very happy, normal life," he explained, "but you will always have to gear things a little slower for her. Perhaps the best way to think of it is to consider her a year or so younger than she actually is. If you will do this, I think that she will move along very nicely."

The parents were indeed grateful for this professional help. Because they had come to understand their daughter's ability, they were better able to meet her needs.

Some children, on the other hand, are unusually gifted intellectually.° Classroom teachers are often at a loss as to what to do with such children. An unusually bright child may be so advanced and may ask so many difficult questions that he becomes a threat to his teacher. Another gifted child, however, may have little or no interest in school work and may want to pursue his own interests. He is often labeled as "lazy" when actually, he is bored.

Sometimes a special problem develops when an unusually bright youngster reaches his teens. Because his interests may be more academic than those of his classmates, he may not find much interest in youth activities. Because of his advanced knowledge and interest in adult affairs, he may bypass many of the social activities which would help him adjust and learn to get along with other young people. Gifted teen-agers, especially girls, often find others their own age uninteresting. They may prefer dating boys older than they.

Another social adjustment confronting the advanced teen-ager is the fact that he may be as much as two years younger than his classmates. Although this may not have presented any problem in the lower grades, because the teen years represent the change from childhood to adulthood, the gap seems much greater. Gifted adults, especially men, often remark that when they were in high school they felt out of place because they were younger than their classmates.

Physical Problems

The physical problems which a person can see are usually the easiest to do something about. Those that are hidden are the ones that give the real trouble. Today, psychologists are learning more about these hidden problems. In

---

°For a more complete discussion on giftedness, see the author's small book, *Is Your Child Gifted?*

years past, they were often stymied. For example, in studying a child they would learn that his school situation was good,
the home environment was excellent, and the child had not
experienced any serious or traumatic experiences. Yet he was
laden with problems. But now, due to much research, it is
known that such children may be suffering from glandular
disfunctions, neurological impairments or other such physical disabilities.

Some years ago, I received a letter from a Christian lady
in which she described her son. It was such a classic example
of a subtly-hidden problem that I kept it in my file:

"We have a precious little boy whom we adopted. He
has been with us since he was only a year old, so you see, we
really are his mommy and daddy and we both love him very
much. It is amazing how much he resembles his younger
brother who is not adopted. They look more alike than some
twins.

"But, with all the love he receives, somewhere along the
line, we must have failed, since he has many problems and he
does so poorly in school — both in his subjects and his social
adjustments. He's had trouble since the start. He has always
been so wiggly. I even had trouble dressing him when he was
a baby. He just couldn't hold still that long, and he was into
something *all* the time.

"He was having such a rough time in school that we had
him retained in the second grade, but he didn't catch up at
all. We had him tutored — but to no avail. We had the school
counselor check him, and he found his I.Q. to be the middle
of the normal range, so we were told he should at least be
able to keep up with his class. His teacher this year told us,
'About the only thing he does well, is to disrupt the class.'

"He shows no interest in anything except play. He can't
accept any responsibility or discipline in any form, and he
has absolutely no self control. He has tantrums when he
doesn't get his own way, and he fights everything — home-
work, eating, sleeping, even going to the bathroom at times
. . . in fact, life in general. He does everything the hard way.
He fights life.

"I'm not nearly the patient, softspoken mother I long to
be, but I try with all my might to be patient with him and I
pray constantly that God will give me the patience and wisdom I so desperately need to raise this little child of His.

The counselor told us that he is very egocentric, yet full of love at times.

"The counselor and his teachers have told us all the things that are wrong with him *but no one seems to know how to remedy the situation.* We neither ask, nor expect him to be an outstanding student. The important thing is that he learn to behave himself, so he'll grow up to be a good, honest person.

"He has been brought to Sunday school and church since he was just a tiny baby. He also belongs to Cub Scouts and I've served as den mother. His father and he belong to Indian Guides, so you see, we try to do things with him and for him.

"Please, how *do* we unlock this door? I'll be prayerfully awaiting an answer. If you have a prayer group that meets, would you please remember us in prayer? I know that all things are possible with God and I truly believe that He is interested in this problem that confronts us every day."

I read the letter carefully, then listed some of the symptoms and situations described:

(1) does poor work in school
(2) problem has persisted for years
(3) hyperactive
(4) situation unchanged by school retention
(5) tutoring to no avail
(6) average I.Q.
(7) disrupts class
(8) interested only in play
(9) won't accept responsibility
(10) discipline problem
(11) no self control
(12) temper tantrums
(13) fights everything
(14) egocentric
(15) lovable at times
(16) no one has remedy
(17) raised in Sunday school and church
(18) belongs to Cub Scouts and Indian Guides

As I looked back over the list, I realized that many of the symptoms form a syndrome which is often found in children who have sustained a brain damage. I wrote to the

mother, suggesting that she contact a neurologist. I also
added that he would probably give balance tests and electro-
encephalogram (brain wave test).

Some months later, she wrote again saying that they
had seen a neurologist who had given a brain wave test and
had confirmed the suspicion that the boy was brain dam-
aged. The injury, the physician felt, may have occurred at
the time of birth. The mother went on to say that the doctor
had prescribed medication which had helped to quiet him
sufficiently to permit him to get on with the business of living without undue stress. The teachers at school were also
alerted to the boy's problem. Now that they understood,
they were more patient and used different teaching techniques which would be more appropriate for him.*

There are many children whose behavior problems are
the result of hidden physical problems. When a child's actions are not consistent with his home background and training, and when behavior problems persist over a long period
of time, it is advisable to seek professional help.

Some physical disabilities are much more apparent. Yet,
children who are so afflicted may attempt to hide their physical weaknesses. This is especially true of those who suffer
with sight or hearing impairment. In fact, some children
manage to slip through school without even revealing their
handicaps. No one realizes that they are laboring under an
extensive loss of one of their senses. If these youngsters *are*
discovered, they are often embarrassed and try to compensate for their disabilities in various ways. Many times the
compensation takes the form of undesirable behavior.

In writing about her thirteen-year-old son, one mother
describes the problems that accompany such a physical
defect:

> "Our son, Curtis, thirteen, is conscientious about his
> school work and does well. He is also conscientious about
> going to church. He has asked Jesus to come into his heart
> and I am sure he is saved. Our son reads a lot, but he plays
> actively, too. He is a happy boy, and is content to play alone.

---

*For a helpful study of brain-injured children, see: *The Brain-Injured
Child* by Richard S. Lewis, Grune and Stratton, Inc. 1951.

"He has been under doctor's care for years and last summer had an operation on his ear. Difficulty comes when his 'good' ear closes with a cold and he must go to school with deafness. His teachers are all cooperative, but Curtis' attitude is not right. He doesn't face the fact that he has a disability, that people are bound to know it, that he has to get along temporarily without hearing well, and that he must do the best he can. The doctor is usually able to open the ear tube and he has no trouble in the summer. He is very much afraid of being laughed at. But this is a cruel world and he will never be happy if he's sorry for himself.

"If he would only let people know he can't hear well, the children wouldn't laugh or stare. But he will not tell even his best friends. His teachers have all said that he gets along well with others. When I remind him of people who have overcome much greater difficulties, he doesn't like it. Do you have any suggestions as to how I can help my son to accept his deafness?"

Curtis' mother shows real insight and understanding. However, she may need to work with her son for some time before he learns to accept his hearing loss. This is understandable. It is a hard thing for an adult to accept a disability, but it is even more difficult for an adolescent. Curtis is undergoing physical and emotional changes. He is no longer a child, but neither is he a grown man. Life is complicated enough as it is without adding something else — a hearing problem. At Curtis' age, he considers it extremely important to be thought well of and to be accepted by his peers. Any chance of losing his status must be avoided. Since adolescents (boys especially) place great stress on physical prowess, a physical disability such as Curtis' is a crushing blow. He considers it a weakness so he feels he must conceal it from his age-mates. Curtis may be wrong about this, but at the present time, he cannot help it.

If Curtis' mother continues to be understanding and kind, he will improve as he grows and matures. In time, he will be secure enough to recognize real values. He will know then that a handicap does not denote weakness. In fact, when a person learns to take his disabilities in stride and make the best of them, it is an indication of strength.

The letter stated that Curtis' hearing loss had occurred

only a little over a year ago. As time goes on, Curtis will become more accustomed to his handicap and he will not be as concerned about it.

It takes time and patience to help a child learn to accept a physical problem. But when he does, this maturity may pave the way for him to fully accept all of his strengths and his weaknesses.

Emotional Problems

Just as we have physical needs that must be cared for, so we have emotional needs which must be fulfilled if we are to be normal, well-adjusted people. Take, for example, the need for love and affection. From the time a baby lets out his first cry until, as an elderly man, he leaves this world, he has a craving for love. If this need is not met, especially when he is young, he will invent numerous mechanisms to compensate for the lack. At first these bids for attention, or personal hurts may seem mild. A child may become a "show-off," strike out at other children, or pull into his shell when he feels he is not wanted or appreciated. Many behavior problems stem from such inner feelings. If his emotional needs are not met, these symptoms will become more pronounced by the time he is an adolescent. If they remain unmet by the time he is an adult, he will often shock society with his bizarre behavior. These extreme actions may take the form of hostile acts or, on the other hand, they may be recognized as severe symptoms of withdrawal. Our penitentiaries and mental institutions are filled with people who have acted out their emotional deprivations on society.

Since emotional needs are often tied in with physical and mental problems, it is not surprising that a person's behavior is often complex and difficult to understand.

Here, for example, is a letter about a child who is evidently quite disturbed and whose aunt is unable to understand why he "acts that way."

"Could you give me some advice concerning my young nephew who is living with us? He is a bright boy but very bull-headed. He wants to obey only at his convenience. He lies to me, and thinks nothing of it. For example, I will give him 25 cents for the Sunday school offering, but instead of giving it in Sunday school, he will go to the candy store and spend it for candy, then give only a nickel in Sunday school. When I ask him, 'did you give the quarter in the offering plate?'

'Yes, Auntie,' he says with a sincere face.

'Well, where did you get the candy?'

'Some boy gave it to me,' or 'I found it.'

"When asked, 'Are you telling the truth?' again with a very sincere face, 'Yes, Auntie, I'm not lying.'

"I would really have to believe him if I hadn't caught him right in the act of spending the money. Upon questioning him as to why he does it (since he really is not in want or need for anything), he simply shrugs his shoulders and says, 'I don't know.'

"In Sunday school his teachers complain to me saying that John isn't bad and he isn't good. He just makes a nuisance of himself. He won't sit quietly, and does things to make the other children laugh. He has been severely punished by spanking, taking certain privileges away, making him go to bed without supper, but all seem to help only for a day or so and then the same thing is repeated again.

"Every night we kneel together and pray, and he always asks Jesus to come into his heart and make him a better boy. Yet there is no improvement. I have tried everything I know, and have not been successful. Now I've come to the end. Is there any help for such a child? His father was just like him when he was little, and still is today. He knows the Gospel but has never given his life to the Lord. Could the boy have inherited this nature? Is there no deliverance for such cases?"

A surface glance does not give much indication as to the boy's real problem. His actions are puzzling until one probes more deeply and uncovers the fact that his basic emotional needs have been neglected throughout his young life. Among other things, he undoubtedly feels the lack of loving parents. No mention is made of his mother, and evidently his father does not live with him either. With such a situation, problems are bound to show up.

Part of this boy's problem may also be attributed to a spiritual lack in his life. He, like everyone else, has a bent for sinning. After he is led into a personal relationship with

Christ and is taught in the Word, he will gradually change and grow in the image of our Lord.

"Why does this boy act as he does?" There are undoubtedly a number of reasons in addition to the spiritual aspects. In the last part of her letter, the aunt asked, "Is there any help for such a child?" Yes, there is. But it requires action. Several sessions with a Christian psychologist, giving appropriate tests, discussing the situation and working through on the various aspects of the boy's problem, would enable this lady to gain insight into her nephew's behavior. As she learns to recognize his emotional needs, she then can help to meet them.

As a child grows older and begins to travel through the adolescent years, he may encounter a number of difficult situations which have not arisen before. The fact that a teen-ager is beginning to assume adult responsibilities and to gain more personal freedom may cause some of these problems. The fact, too, that he is becoming sexually mature may also cause some erratic behavior. These are often problem days, and most families with teen-agers experience at least some growing pains. To heap on rules and regulations is a superficial way of handling teen-age problems and usually has no lasting value.

In fact, cold requirements without the warmth of love and understanding may only aggravate an already tense situation. Such a strain often results in widening the gap between parents and child, and the method of control overshadows the real needs of a teen-ager. This is true of the mother who wrote the following letter about her teen-age daughter:

"Our daughter is 15 years old. We haven't allowed her to start dating yet.

"She has been liking a boy for three years and lately he gave her his ring to wear around her neck, signifying they were going steady. When I found this out, I made her give the ring right back and told her she was too young to even think about going steady. I want her to be friendly, but not flirtatious.

"In a few weeks she met another boy and took his ring, again saying, 'I'm going steady.' When I found out about this,

I became very provoked and we had an unpleasant scene. I caught her in several lies so I put her on a month's restriction, forbidding her to receive any telephone calls from this boy. However, this was really no punishment for her because she saw him every day at school anyway. Finally, before the month was up, the boy called and lied to me about who he was. She talked to him, and then she lied to me and told me it was a girl calling.

"I had kept all this from her daddy because he isn't understanding with her, but I told her I would turn it over to him since she neither obeyed me nor stayed away from the boy. So we all three got together and I let her tell her daddy the whole story.

"I was surprised! *What he said to her did more harm than good.* When we didn't get anywhere with our daughter, I thought it would help if my husband talked to her boyfriend, but it didn't do any good. Things are now as bad as they were at the beginning, and in some ways worse! She doesn't have his ring anymore, but in her heart she says she's still going steady.

"What can you do about a problem like this? She sees the boy every day at school. She has become so distant to me. She stays in her room with the door closed, listens to the radio (this popular trash) and I don't seem to be able to reach her at all.

"Is there anything I can do? She accuses me of not understanding. Do you think I have handled this in the wrong way?"

This is a complicated situation and an unhappy one for all involved. The mother, who evidently has always controlled the girl by strict discipline, now discovers that she is ignored and overruled. The father seems to be left out completely, except as a measure of last resort. Then his only role seems to be that of a "policeman" to enforce the law. The daughter, on the other hand, feels that she is misunderstood and treated unfairly. Whereas she was submissive and had always obeyed when she was younger, she now feels that she is old enough to make decisions for herself. Although she rebels against the rigid control of her mother by disregarding her commands, she is undoubtedly filled with feelings of guilt and insecurity — guilt, because she has disobeyed, and insecurity because she has lost the favor of her mother.

This problem is intensified because the lines of communication are closed between the family members. If they had been able to discuss the problem freely in a friendly manner, much of the difficulty might have been resolved. As it is, the walls of resentment are being built higher, and communication is becoming more difficult.

It is apparent that the mother has been concentrating on the girl's disobedience rather than on the problem which triggered it. Although the mother's concern was for her daughter's own personal good, she permitted rules and regulations to stand in the way of reaching her own child. If the mother could back off and view the problem from a different perspective, she might see that if, over the years, she had given her daughter more *love* rather than control, the girl might not now be searching for love and appreciation from another source.

Children *do* need regulations, but such are ineffective when they become a barrier between parent and child. Teen-agers need parental control and guidance, but it is most effective when accompanied by love and understanding. When the relationship remains a pleasant one, it is not difficult for parents to obtain the cooperation they are seeking.

One of the most common causes of problems that beset boys and girls is a disrupted home. This may be the result of the death of one or more of the parents, or it may be caused by divorce or separation. In any case, the child suffers a severe loss which often affects his behavior and social adjustment.

While visiting recently at the Menninger Foundation in Topeka, Kansas, I talked with the staff of psychiatrists at the out-patient clinic for adults. "What," I asked, "are the childhood experiences that seem especially devastating and which cause people to have serious mental problems as adults?" The group thought for a minute, then brought out the fact that many of their patients had histories of broken homes. Indeed children do suffer from losing and changing parents.

Children, like the one discussed in the following letter,

who have had to "change horses in the middle of a stream," find it difficult to adjust.

"I have known Jesus as my personal Saviour for two years now. Since then, my thinking and views on things have changed.

"Three years ago I married a divorced man with two children. I was only 17. One of the children, Christine, now ten years old, accepted the Lord a year ago. She has always been a problem. Furthermore, my husband and I don't agree on discipline. I love the child and I feel that she loves me. But she does all sorts of things to get attention. Now she is lying and won't admit that she is wrong.

"Her teacher wants us to send her to a psychologist. My husband, however, is against it. After much prayer I feel the Lord has told me to wait. There is no *Christian* psychologist in this area anywhere. Is there anything I can do?"

If Christine had not had to change parents, she might have had some problems anyway. But living for a time without a mother, then making a complete change when she was only seven years of age, undoubtedly placed a burden upon her which she has not known how to handle. What her father told her about her natural mother, we do not know. We do know that when she walked into this new family arrangement at seven, she found that she had a mother who was only a teen-ager herself. For some time Christine may have been the apple of her father's eye. But when her father remarried, she was required to share his affection with a seventeen-year-old bride. In addition, the teen-aged step-mother may have had so many problems of her own that she could not take time to attend to Christine's. It takes unusual wisdom for a step-mother to win her place as the family's new "mother." And it takes time. The children are apt to resent discipline, thinking, "My real mother wouldn't treat me like this." To make matters worse, the new mother may have felt that she needed to prove herself to her husband by "disciplining the kids." If so, you can imagine how Christine reacted. The writer admitted that she and her husband didn't agree on discipline. Hence, we have two girls, one seven and another, her step-mother, seventeen, both going through times of transition and both undoubtedly fighting for survival. Indeed it is difficult to understand the feelings of a child who comes from a broken home.

Another concern which some mothers experience is that of their sons' or daughters' romances. One of the greatest heartbreaks in life is to raise a child until the teen-age years, then to see her throw herself away into a poor marriage. Although friends and other onlookers may wonder why parents don't cut the strings and let their son or daughter alone now that he or she is married, it really isn't that simple. A parent can't cut off the emotional ties in a few weeks or even months simply because his daughter ran off to a justice of the peace and signed some papers. This is the problem which faced the mother who wrote the following letter:

"Our teen-age daughter has always had only one goal in life: to be married. She was a good student and her teachers tried to get her to go on to college. They felt she had the ability to make a fine teacher. However, she seemed to fall head over heels in love with every boy that she dated. She has been engaged twice and was informally engaged another time. Her last engagement ended in marriage.

"We feel our daughter has made a mistake. She was not content at home. We feel she would have married almost anyone just to be married. The fellow she married is what I'd call an 'odd ball.' You talk to him and maybe he will answer and maybe he won't. He told our daughter he didn't believe in wasting words. If he didn't feel a question was important, he just didn't answer. He said he had seen people talk all afternoon and say nothing worthwhile. Yet, he has our daughter convinced that he is very brilliant.

"We told her this kind of man wouldn't fit into our family since we are a close family and love to get together for the holidays. A holiday has just passed, and our family got together. She and her husband came but didn't visit with anyone — just sat off by themselves. They didn't seem to care for the rest of us.

"How long can she stand such a secluded life? He almost never mentions his parents. Now our daughter seldom writes or visits us. He knows we did not approve of this marriage. We felt that if our daughter cared enough, she'd at least come to visit us.

"We have been deeply hurt. As most parents, we wanted a

happy marriage for our daughter. We would like to have had a son-in-law we could enjoy being with, and one we could be proud of. We would appreciate your suggestions."

Perhaps one of the healthy signs of this problem is that the mother is not withholding her true feelings. Rather, she is ventilating them and getting them out in the open where she can analyze and deal with them. How much better this is than to muffle them within her where they are likely to crop out again in the form of physical complications or even severe depression.

It is quite apparent that the daughter was never very happy when at home with her parents. If she had been satisfied there, she would not have been so anxious to leave home and jump into just any marriage. Now that she is away from her parents and is married to a man her parents feel is an "odd ball," they seem to be disappointed that she gives no evidence of being happy. It is interesting, too, that the mother had wanted her daughter's husband to fit closely into their family unit, when obviously the daughter did not enjoy real communication at home even before she left. Although the causes may not be recognizable on the surface, it would seem by the girl's actions that she harbored resentment against her parents. The mother states that for years the daughter had wanted to get away from home. Why, we do not know. It may have been that her parents were too critical, too demanding, or that they tried to control her life. If any of these situations existed, it is understandable why the girl is not anxious to spend time at home. Yet, her mother is hurt because her daughter does not come to visit them more.

Actually, the girl's actions are quite consistent. That is, for years, she has wanted to leave the family and now that she has left, she doesn't seem especially interested in coming back.

We can sympathize with the mother in her deep feelings for her daughter. However, she and all other mothers do have an adequate resource in the Lord Jesus Christ. When discouraged parents take their problems to the Lord, and leave them with Him, they are never disappointed.

Christ truly understands our hearts and He is waiting to meet every need of our lives.

CHAPTER TEN

Extra Family Members

A wedding is always lovely, but Charlotte's was especially so. The strains from the organ were soft and sweet. The candelabra shed a romantic glow as the bridesmaids moved slowly down the aisle.

Then came Charlotte, a picture of loveliness in her white satin gown. All eyes were fixed on her radiant face. The handsome groom stood near the altar, and the fragrant aroma of the flowers filled the sanctuary.

Soon the congregation would hear them say, "I do."

What Charlotte did not realize that day, was that she was saying "I do" to family members other than her husband.

Today, years later, she knows there is more to her marriage than she bargained for.

Shortly after they were married, Charlotte's father-in-law moved in for what was to be a "few weeks." But the weeks dragged into months and the months into years while the headaches increased. Her husband was a Christian, clean in his habits and mature in his actions. But his father was hardly the same kind of person. He had his favorite television programs and no one dared to interfere with his line up of shows for the evening.

He had definite attitudes on politics, religion and women. Unfortunately, instead of leaving the room when another couple came over, he would move to center stage and air his pet theories on government and all else.

Charlotte knew that Cecil's dad was hurting their marriage, but what could she do? It wasn't that Cecil's dad was so bad, it was just that he was one person too many in their marriage. This was especially true at the dinner table at night. There were so many things she wanted to discuss with her husband. But there was his dad, all ears and with a ready opinion. It was just too much. She had about all she could take. How she wished that she and Cecil could just live their lives together. But with someone else in the house, she was always on guard and unsettled.

She tried to be understanding and remember that he *was* Cecil's dad, but her patience was wearing pretty thin. It seemed to her that Cecil should see that his dad was intruding. Yet, so far there were no signs that he realized it at all.

Charlotte did not want to hurt Cecil. She loved him and wanted him to be happy. So she just suffered in silence, but it did strain their relationship with each other. Naturally, the children were affected, too.

Charlotte's situation is not uncommon. Women everywhere are writing about similar problems. This is a situation one woman described:

> "My father-in-law lives with us and he does things that are very embarrassing. I tell my husband it is his place to talk to him. It seems as though my husband thinks he may hurt his father's feelings and therefore affect his health.

> "He is also very contrary about meals. I think things would be fine if my husband would just sit down and tell him 'what is what' and that there are just some things he won't put up with. Instead, when I go to him about these things he flies into a rage and tells me I won't have him much longer (he is 80 years old).

> "He has lived with us 14 years out of the 17 years we have been married. Recently, when my husband and I have talked, it has brought on a serious argument. I feel it is time now to make other arrangements. But I know if I suggest that, it will bring on more trouble.

> "There are two other sons and two daughters in the family. I feel something could be worked out, but my husband's sister has told me he couldn't live with them because her husband was too nervous to put up with him. But what about *our* home and the happiness of *our* children? My husband's brothers can't be bothered, either. Please tell me, am I wrong or is it my place to take things good-naturedly? This man is wrecking our home and our happiness."

Another woman has much the same problem with her own father who is living with them. She refers to him as a tyrant:

"How do you react to a father who has been a selfish tyrant with his children all his life? Now he is old and still at it. He lives with us but has never accepted the fact that I am married. He doesn't like my husband; just tolerates him. At Christmas time, he just sits down to receive gifts, but he gives nothing, although he has a bank account. As a matter of fact, he has more money than we do. He expects gifts of at least $10.00 or more, rather more. If I don't jump when he gives an order, I get a nasty, sarcastic lecture. He is not a Christian and has one of the most terrible dispositions I've ever seen. He is about to drive the children crazy.

"I am trying to live a Christian life. What do I do now?"

Bruce had a similar problem but, in his case, it was his mother-in-law. Little did he realize when he and Suzie were married that her mother would occupy a central position in their marriage. A few weeks afterward, he got some indication of what was ahead when his wife innocently remarked, "Oh, I always share everything with mother. I always have." And she said it in a way that indicated she *always intended* to share everything with her. That is to say everything in their marriage was to be cleared with mother.

This annoyed Bruce. He had played quarterback on his high school football team and he wasn't used to having someone else call the signals for him. He figured that his marriage was his business and he could call his own plays. He wasn't about to let his wife's mother send in plays from the bench and even worse, take over his quarterback position.

He told Suzie so. She blew up and called him a dictator. He took it from there and for two days they hardly spoke. But she spoke plenty with her mother. He got the idea that they were having "fried Bruce" several times a day. He began to feel like an outsider. And he was. Suzie was still married to her mother.

But what could Bruce do? He loved Suzie. She was active in the church and a wonderful girl. There never would be anyone else but her. The pathetic part is that in

Suzie's case, she does not even know that she is tied to her mother. The conditioning has been so subtle through the years that her dependence is purely unconscious. This is the worst kind. She has been a leaner so long that she is unaware of her leaning. But Bruce is aware of it. If she must lean on someone, that is where he comes in. He cannot but resent anyone else, even a mother, coming between him and his wife.

In Bernice's case, she knows that she is tied to her mother. She wishes it were not so but she knows it is. She is aware that her mother's dominance in her marriage is disturbing her relationship with her husband but she seems powerless to handle the situation. What can she do? She loves her mother. *Her mother has always been so good to her.* After all, what else can a daughter ask of her mother? What is she supposed to do? Tell her to take off and stay out of her life? No, that would break her mother's heart.

Another frequent type of in-law problem is that which arises between a wife and her mother-in-law. Such tangles are never completely lopsided, but the woman who interferes with her son's happy marriage usually has no leg to stand on. Another young woman tells her story in the following letter:

"When my husband and I were making plans for our wedding, I first met his parents. Since they lived some distance away, I looked forward to meeting Pete's mother. I had not been raised in a Christian home, so I felt I could learn a great deal from her.

"When I met her she said, 'hello' but only glanced at me, and never smiled. She said she couldn't understand what her son saw in me. Now she lives with us.

"We have been married for eight years and I've never seen her really happy or joyful. She always looks on the dark side of things. She finds something wrong with everything. She is always sick and I really believe there is nothing wrong with her. She has been in and out of hospitals but the doctor finds nothing physically wrong. I've heard her say, 'If you are sick in body, this means you are closer to the Lord.' As a sign of her righteousness she quotes, 'The just shall be afflicted.'

"She is rude to people, and gossips. She is continually

bragging on herself. My husband and I have taken her on trips, bought her things, and spent much time remodeling her home. Yet she has turned others against us. She has become a stumbling block to me instead of a blessing. I fret about this and become very depressed since I have to live with this.

"How can I be right with God when I hold evil thoughts about her in my mind? I have an urge to strike back because of the trouble she has caused. Sometimes I wish she was out of my way. I guess what I really want is for her to admit just once she isn't perfect, then apologize for hurting my feelings. She does things to make me angry, then points her finger at me and says, 'See, you're mad and I'm not. I don't get mad.'

"When I look at my mother-in-law all I see is sorrow, complaining, nagging and bragging. I'm sick of it, but I can't change her, so I guess I must change myself. How can I overcome this?"

Many of the women who write our office point out the effect an in-law is having on their *children*. The adults can put up with the problem, but the children are caught in the currents of opposite opinion and emotional conflict. They know that the unhealthy emotional climate that is created in the home may cause their children to go through life with deep personality scars. The following letter expresses a mother's concern for her children:

"I am a young Christian mother and am so anxious to give my family the right kind of home life.

"Do you have any booklet on mother-in-law difficulties? Although I know I am a Christian, it seems to be very hard to display love toward my mother-in-law. I have to pray constantly, to keep a sweet attitude. I feel I can hardly stand another moment.

"She is a Christian also and that causes me to wonder how she can be so hateful. I have been married for nine years now. I've tried being patient, loving, kind, but nothing seems to work. She is bossy, dominant, possessive and talkative. She quotes the Bible continually to prove her point, but little does she know how disturbed she is. And what makes it worse, *my husband is so used to it, he doesn't know the difference.*

"I know it has been God who has been my strength during these testing times. If you have any suggestions on how to get along with a husband's mother, I would greatly appreciate this. I have failed somewhere. *My greatest concern though, is for the children.* My mother-in-law is a law unto herself, and she is in constant conflict with the children. They try to be polite to her, but inside they boil. I know this is not good for them, but neither do I know what to do."

The kinds of problems which extra family members bring to a home are endless. These difficulties may affect the children, the husband, or wife in various ways. Occasionally a person writes about an in-law who is setting a bad and embarrassing moral example for all concerned. This letter is typical of some I receive:

"My husband and I have been married six years and have two daughters. I was brought up in a Christian home, but my husband was not. We are both Christians now and are doing our best to bring our children up in a Christian environment.

"My husband's mother, a divorcee, lives with us. She is a dear person who doesn't smoke or drink and has always been good to us. She is thoughtful and kind, but she is *not* a Christian. Therefore, she is doing something that hurts us deeply. She is having an affair with a married man and this has been going on for several years.

"We do so want to win her to Christ, but it seems as though we are getting nowhere. Our older son said to her one day, 'Grandma, why don't you send Neal home to his own family?'

"The children love her but we don't approve of what she is doing. Yet, we don't want to turn our children against her. But neither do we want them to think it is right to live a flagrantly immoral life.

"What do you think is the best approach to this problem?"

Fortunately, not all people who live with others are causing problems. Many people are ready to stand up and tell of relatives such as grandparents, mothers or fathers-in-law, uncles or aunts, and other extra family members who have been a great blessing in the home. In fact, one of the greatest blessings in life can result from someone who lives in with a family. But to do so requires real insight and interpersonal skills.° One woman, for example, told of the bless-

---

°For a copy of the booklet, "How to Live Successfully with Relatives," write the author, Box 206, Pasadena, California.

ing of her mother-in-law in the home. The wife was unsaved and quite uninterested in "religion." But her husband and her mother-in-law knew the Saviour. "Because of Mom's beautiful life and her sensitivity to my wishes in the family," said the wife, "I finally became interested in her Lord. In time I gave my heart to Christ. I'll always be grateful to Mom for what she did for our family."

People who live in with others do not have it easy either. A multitude of problems and misunderstandings rear their ugly heads to cause hard feelings. And it takes all the wisdom and spirituality an in-law can muster up in order to make things go smoothly.

The Aging Process

Many of the letters about extra family members which come to my desk concern men and women who are advanced in years. "She's critical and hard to live with," they say. What the writer does not understand is that this parent may actually be senile and not responsible for her actions. Some parents reach advanced years without much loss of physical vigor and mental alertness. Others, however, begin to show signs of senility at a surprisingly early age. In some persons the blood is unable to carry the necessary nourishment to the brain cells, resulting in various symptoms of senility. They appear to be normal in most ways, yet act childlike in others. It is much easier to be patient with an older person if it is known that he has become senile and is actually not accountable for his actions.

Georgia, for example, was very happy when she learned that her mother-in-law, an elderly woman, who lived across the country, would be coming to visit them. But Georgia had not seen her mother-in-law for years, and when she arrived it soon became apparent that her stay was going to be unpleasant. Three times a day the mother-in-law would quiz Georgia about plans for the meal. "Well, I'm sorry you are going to have that," she said, "because I don't like that at all. Do you have any cereal? If you do, fix me a bowl of cereal. I need all the vitamins and proteins that come with it."

Georgia looked at her in amazement and, of course, was disappointed that she wouldn't eat the food she had prepared. After several days, Georgia gave up, and asked her husband how long his mother was going to stay. "I can't do anything to please her," Georgia said.

Each afternoon the mother-in-law would become nervous and demand that Georgia take her for a ride. But once in the car, the mother-in-law's favorite warning was, "Don't hit that car! Don't hit that car! I think you're getting too close now. You're liable to hit that car!"

At long last the day arrived when the mother-in-law would take the plane back home. Although the departure was not scheduled until 4:00 o'clock in the afternoon, and the airport was only a short distance from their home, the mother-in-law got up at 5:00 a.m. and began "shooing" the family around. "I'm afraid we'll be late," she urged. After Georgia explained that they would not have to go to the airport until nine hours later, the mother-in-law finally settled down for a bite of breakfast. But throughout the day she kept asking about the time.

"I thought I would go crazy," Georgia said later. "I suppose if she asked me once, she asked me a thousand times if it was time to go to the airport." Finally, Georgia and her husband took her two hours earlier than necessary, simply to put their departing guest at ease. But this was not the end of their trials and tribulations. When they drove up to the airport two hours in advance, "mama" jumped out of the car, ran into the terminal, by-passed all of the passengers who were standing in line and demanded that they give her a ticket right away.

When the two returned home they almost fell in a faint. "I have never been so exhausted in all my life," said Georgia. "I know just how you feel," agreed her husband.

What Georgia and her husband did not realize was that this woman had become senile and was not altogether responsible. In fact, not long afterward, she became so severe that she had to be hospitalized.

Dramas like these are not uncommon. Many women are trying to cope with an elderly mother or father who actually needs special medical care. During the past generation, life expectancy has become much greater, but with this extension of life come problems such as senility which cannot be overlooked.

Cultural Differences

Sometimes the presence of a parent or an in-law causes a subtle problem which a couple may not have identified or discussed. It concerns the cultural backgrounds of a husband and wife.

For example, Lola Smith and Albert Jones came from very different backgrounds, but this didn't keep them from falling in love and getting married. Then came the rub. Each thought that his own family's way of doing things was just right, and each was loathe to forsake the traditions of his family. Everything probably would have worked out, except that after a year of marriage, Lola's mother came to live with them. Shortly after she moved in, Albert saw things were now going to be done the "Smith" way. This was only natural because Lola's mother reinforced all that Lola believed and felt. But what made it worse was this: As soon as their first child was born, Lola and her mother began their indoctrination of Albert, Jr. Nearly all he learned was a direct reflection of the Smith's way of doing things.

Poor Albert didn't stand a chance. Although he never came right out and told them, he felt deeply that as long as his mother-in-law was in his house, his own children would never have the benefit of learning and doing things the way he had in *his* home. In short, he felt rejected and felt that he had lost his own son.

If Lola and Albert had not brought an extra family member into the home, they undoubtedly would have worked out a compromise. The best of the Smiths and the best of the Joneses would have eventually blended to produce their *own* family's traditions — ones which would have made them both proud and happy. As it was, Albert felt that not only had the traditions of his family been rejected, but he had, too. Consequently, as a "third party" he had little incentive to make the marriage work.

Attachments

When a husband or wife becomes attached to a family member other than his mate, it is usually (1) a mother (2) a father (3) brothers and sisters or (4) the parent family in general. The apron strings may have been tied so early and so subtly that they weren't even noticeable to the person himself.

Although some girls are closely attached to their fathers, this is usually not the case. The fact that a father has to detach himself from the home sufficiently to leave the house during the day to make a living for the family, usually means that there is little opportunity for a daughter to become too dependent on her father.

Other unhealthy attachments may involve two or more sisters. Because a wife, as a child, may have grown up with and associated closely with her sisters, there may be an especially strong attachment even in adulthood. Many husbands resent the fact that their wives seem to have more loyalty to their sisters than to their own husbands.

Sometimes a husband or wife is not attached merely to one person in the family but to the *parental family in general.* A child may grow up believing that his or her family is almost sacred. Although the sons and daughters of that family may get married, they never think of themselves as leaving the original family. Instead, they think of themselves as going out, finding a mate, *then bringing this mate back into the family fold.* As a result, they have a greater loyalty and attachment to their parental family than to the new family being formed by marriage.

It is not unusual to find a husband who has a strong attachment to his father. He may feel that his father is his "pal" and understanding companion. This overly-strong attachment is strengthened even more if the husband feels that his wife does not understand him. "At least my Dad understands," he feels.

As a Christian wife, try to back off, stand on a little hill as it were, and gain a true perspective of your relationship with your parents and siblings. You are fortunate indeed if you are a woman who has happy, close ties with your own family. Yet in your marriage, it is vitally important to keep at least one eye on the fact that cords that bind too closely to the "old nest" may keep you from being your best in a new one.

Astrid had not assumed her new name, "Mrs. Sutter," long before she realized that there was another Mrs. Sutter who was very dominant in her husband's life —his mother. Soon Astrid learned that her place as Ted's wife was secondary to his mother's.

"What's wrong with me?" she wondered. "What causes Ted to go to his mother?" Astrid felt left out and annoyed and jealous. It was anything but a good basis for a happy marriage. Although she didn't say much, Astrid's feelings began to show themselves in physical symptoms. She developed headaches, depression and other somatic complaints.

This, however, works both ways. A husband may feel rejected and threatened or inadequate when his wife gives stronger allegiance to some other family member than she does to him. In some instances he may seek affection and solace from another. This is what happened to Doris' husband, Vernon. Although Doris did not realize it, through the years he learned that he could not compete with her mother, to whom she was strongly attached. No matter what Vernon said, he was always wrong. He could never win because there were two on the other side. If the extra party had been a man, Vernon could have taken care of the situation. If his wife were alone, he could have reasoned things through. But as it was, he felt helpless.

Finally Vernon began turning to an alternate woman. Not that he wanted to. He knew he was wrong and he always felt guilty about it when he came home. He even prayed and asked God's forgiveness for his straying. But he longed for affection and acceptance, so he would go again.

The plain truth is, blunt and unsavory as it may be, Vernon was finding it easier to find another "wife on the side" than to change his own wife and her mother. Wrong? Yes, it was wrong. But he wasn't the only one who was wrong. Doris, who had promised to put him first was letting him run a slow second to her mother. Emotionally he couldn't take it lying down.

This happens thousands of times. Good men have been emotionally shoved into triangles by the mother-daughter relationship after marriage. Christian counselors meet this situation time and again. A man who is stymied by a wife who is tied to her mother is caught in a dilemma which makes him desperate.

Furthermore, Doris' mother is pretty clever about it. She is more than anxious to baby-sit for them, do the ironing, and many other helpful things. This, she feels, entitles her to speak her piece and throw her weight around. But Vernon sees through this as if it were written on a blackboard. He isn't willing to sell his soul for a baby-sitter, and he resents the fact that he is playing second fiddle to Doris' mother.

What the Bible Teaches

A true Christian is always sensitive to the will of God as revealed in the Bible. Regardless of a woman's attitude toward her mother-in-law, if they are true believers, they want to know what the Word of God teaches. They know that this path is the only one which will eventually lead to blessing.

I am always interested in letters from those who have extra family member problems. I have noticed that although they express giant problems with serious confusion, many of them end something like this: "I do want to please the Lord, though. Please advise me of my Christian obligation."

As in all other matters, the Bible teaching on family living is sane and sensible, and the only one which will really work. Basically, it is this: (1) Leave and cleave (Matthew 19:5) and (2) Honor and care for your parents (I Timothy 5:8).

To *leave and cleave* means to leave one's parents, and cleave to each other. This is the only way a husband and wife can be at their best.

To honor and care for one's parents means to treat them with due regard, and to help meet their needs if this is indicated.

But the Bible does not teach that a husband and a wife should bring extra family members *into their home*.

When we choose our mate and are married, we are to cleave to that person. A woman's husband is to become "first" in her life. There is to be no other person before the one whom you have solemnly taken to be your partner in marriage. No matter how good her parents may have been to her, next to God, her husband should have her allegiance.

Neither are we to forget our parents and to forget the joyous privilege we have of ministering to them in their later years. We can find a place for them where we can see them and help pay for their care. A place where, if necessary, we can watch over them. This is our happy privilege.

Irene's father died when she was in her teens. She was the last child in a family of six children. All the rest were married and gone before she met Art. It was difficult to get married and leave her mother. She told Art so, and he was most understanding. Before they were married, they took Irene's mother with them and went around the neighborhood looking for a small apartment. They found one. Three other Christian women lived in the same apartment building.

It worked out well. Irene's mother had her own friends and enjoyed the freedom of her apartment. She had many good times with Irene and Art, and their relationship was not marred by friction and misunderstanding.

New Facilities for Senior Citizens

With the average life span increasing, there is a great increase in the number of senior citizens. This has alerted many Christian organizations to provide facilities where Christians may retire in surroundings congenial to their Christian faith.

For the Christian couple who has senior in-laws, this can be an excellent solution to the problem of residence. These homes are springing up everywhere, and chances are there are such provisions somewhere near your home.

Those who live in retirement homes know the many benefits. Before long they are part of the new family and enjoy the community living. It is often more satisfactory than trying to become adjusted to the ways and pace of a young couple with children.

The Christian couple can help to share in the expense of such an arrangement, visit the person at his dwelling, and from time to time invite him to their home.

Parents Are Always Parents

Couples who are married should remember that parents are always parents. It is difficult for a dad to forget that Maxine is married and no longer under his care. He feels that he has a right to scold and instruct her, and suffer with her when she is ill even though she does have a husband. She is still his daughter — actually and emotionally. Marriage does not sever the memories of a thousand nights when he kissed her off to sleep. Few saw him wipe away the tears when he realized that his little daughter was toddling right out of his life into the kindergarten and now the teachers will share this little darling of his life. No, a marriage ceremony does not shut off those memories and close out the many happy scenes of her girlhood under his watchful and proud eye.

True, he gave her to that fine young Christian man, but Dad is still emotionally tied by ten thousand ties of love and hallowed memories which cannot be blotted out by a marriage ceremony. She is still his daughter, married or not.

Only a parent knows the aching feeling when one of his children leaves the home nest. Mature as he may be, he is still Dad. Mom is still Mom. Certainly, parents are going to get into their children's hair now and then. They are just parents. Perhaps immature, but nonetheless, parents.

So it demands all the understanding in the world for a married couple to try and climb into the life of a parent or in-law and understand his feelings. Consequently, when we talk of the "intrusion of parents" into the lives of their married children, we walk on sacred ground with tender heart.

But after all this has been said, many couples have proved that it is better whenever possible for a couple to raise their family without extra family members living in the home.

Chapter Eleven

Sex Problems in Marriage

Pastors have often remarked, "I never knew people had so many sex problems until I entered the ministry and started counseling with married couples."

People *do* have endless problems of sex, and counselors know that these problems are usually tied in with other maladjustments. They seldom exist independently.

Since God has made sexual functioning a normal, vital part of life, it cannot be separated from the total personality. In other words, *sex problems are seldom just sex problems.* They are life, personality, attitude problems. When women write me about various problems of sex, they invariably tell about *other* difficulties in marriage. In fact, other maladjustments actually produce sex problems. The following is an example of how sex problems grow out of larger personality conflicts:

"I have a problem of years' standing. I cannot speak to anyone about it and it hounds me every day. I hardly know where to start, but I'll try.

"When I married, I made the mistake of my life. I guess I married to escape an unhappy home. I was too sheltered as a child and was never permitted to grow up in a healthy way. When I left home, I sort of broke away, casting aside all of it. I shouldn't have married my husband. In time, after marriage, I grew up and began to understand myself and my husband.

"Our sex life is terrible. I could write pages and pages and still not tell you how terrible things are. He hasn't the least idea of the true meaning of sex in marriage. When I was first married, my own attitudes weren't too good either. He never satisfies me and he says I never satisfy him. You are probably thinking, 'She's cold and frigid.' But I'm not. *In fact,*

I want love. I feel starved for true love. I'm terribly lonely. I should love him, but I can't."

This information is enough to show that the main problem is not sex. It is ostensibly a long-standing problem on the part of both the wife and the husband. As a result, it is reflected in sexual maladjustments. If both were happy, well-adjusted individuals, they would probably not be complaining of sexual incompatibility. The solution to their problem will come only if each becomes well-adjusted. Then their marriage and their sexual relations will stand a good chance of being satisfactory. This is true of nearly all sex problems. They are reflections of *personality* problems.

The Unsatisfied Wife

One of the strongest desires in a human being is the desire for sexual satisfaction. This is the way God intended it. Like other desires, such as hunger, thirst or sleep, it cries for fulfillment. When satisfaction of the sex urge is thwarted in marriage, frustration and unhappiness result.

There are undoubtedly those who assume that a really spiritual Christian has little interest in sex. But this is unscriptural and surely untrue. A strong sex drive and a strong spiritual life can go along together. For married people, this is the ideal.

Human beings are sexual beings. Sex is ordained of God, and mankind is commanded to be fruitful and replenish the earth. Furthermore, in the New Testament the Apostle Paul encourages believers to have continuing intimate relations, except by mutual consent for a time. Speaking to husbands and wives he says: "Do not refuse and deprive and defraud each other (of your due marital rights), except perhaps by mutual consent for a time, that you may devote yourselves unhindered to prayer. But afterwards resume marital relations, lest Satan tempt you (to sin) through your lack of restraint of sexual desire" (I Corinthians 7:5, *Amplified New Testament*).

This is a good basis for healthy attitudes toward sex. But some men are never able to measure up to God's standard of normal male behavior. Because of certain attitudes and experiences, a husband may not be able to satisfy his wife. As a result, she feels tense, restless and rejected. But her feelings are much deeper than that. She may lose respect for him or, on the other hand, she may turn inward, feeling she is neglected or inadequate herself.

Mary's problem. Mary was not a prude. She was an intelligent Christian woman who prepared for marriage the best she could. She read books about the intimate aspects of marriage, and in every way gained wholesome information. Six months after her marriage she was in tears. She became so upset that she refused to have relations with her husband.

What was her problem? Basically it was her husband's lack of understanding. He had the idea that his own satisfaction was the primary matter in their relationships. As a result, his wife was never satisfied. She would lie awake many nights frustrated and nervous.

Fortunately, her pastor, a man of broad understanding, referred the couple to a marriage counselor who talked with each separately, then together. He showed them charts and made various suggestions. It was somewhat of a blow to the husband's ego, but he cooperated well and he gained much from the sessions. He followed the counsel that was given, and as time passed, they made a much better adjustment.

Colleen's problem. Colleen could not enjoy relations with her husband because she thought they were wrong. She loved Richard, her husband, but sex — no. The whole process seemed like an ordeal.

Colleen's mother, who had been married and divorced twice, had warned her about men. "They are just a bunch of beasts. They think only of one thing, sex." This mother was merely reflecting her own experiences which were real to her.

Finally, Richard blew up. He was a normal, healthy man who felt no guilt at all about sex relations with his wife. And he was faithful to Colleen. There were no other women in his life. But at times, he had to admit, he sort of wished there were. Richard told her she had wrong attitudes and that she'd gotten them from her mother.

Colleen became defensive and said there was nothing wrong with her or her mother that a little gentlemanliness on his part couldn't cure. The argument lasted for months and the tension between them grew.

"The least you could do is read a book on the subject," he argued. Reluctantly Colleen agreed to do so. But after she had read a few pages, she put it down in disgust. But a few days later she read some more. Richard encouraged her, explaining that it was written by a competent doctor and that his pastor had recommended it.

This slowed Colleen down a little. She wanted her marriage to be happy, so she tried to be more open-minded. When Richard saw she was struggling to adopt new ideas, he became very loving and patient. *I guess she's not to blame,* he thought. They were both Christians and recognized that to be married meant they were married for life.

It took time and patience for both Richard and Colleen, but her attitudes finally changed. When they did, she found that her needs were met and that physical relations could be a beautiful legacy of God.

Diana's problem. In high school, Diana dated Ted. He was from an upper class family — sports cars and all. He was student body president, captain of the football team and, to her, the biggest wheel on campus. Diana tells her story in this way:

"What he saw in me, I don't know. I felt so inferior. But I did love him — actually adored him. Right after graduation from high school, we got married. When it came to our sex life, I was really afraid. I guess I was afraid that I could never meet his needs. What happened was that I overdid it. In fact, after a few months I found that he couldn't meet my needs. This puzzled me because he always seemed so masculine.

"As a result of my aggressiveness and sexual demands, I almost ruined a beautiful part of our lives. Naturally, I repulsed Ted, who liked to feel that he was 'the man in charge.'

"Gradually I came to realize that if I were more feminine, less demanding, then my husband would be more attracted to me. This is exactly what has happened. I let my husband do the leading and we are very happy now and our lives are greatly enriched daily by an increased spiritual and physical love."

Experienced counselors know that this is quite often the case when a man seems inadequate. Without realizing it, a wife may do or say things that cause her husband to withdraw. This is frequently adjusted by freer communication, or by patience on the wife's part. It may, however, require professional help.

Arlene's problem

"It seems to me, Dr. Narramore, that you never have received a letter of this nature.

"My husband and I are married for ten years, and during all this time we have never had sexual relations. While we were dating we never mentioned sex. And when we were married, both of us were very ignorant of sex, as neither of our parents had ever discussed things with us. But after some time I began reading books and there I learned that sex is a very basic part of married life. Many times I felt I should talk to my husband about it, but I could never bring myself to do so.

"One day someone came to us and asked us if we would want to adopt an unmarried girl's expectant baby. We agreed to do so, and when her time of delivery came, it was twins. So we adopted them — a boy and a girl. They are three years old now, and we love them very dearly. I couldn't love my own more than I do them. I don't even think about the fact that they are adopted. They are such sweet, lovable little tykes. We got them directly from the hospital. Hardly anyone knows our children are adopted. So here we are, married ten years, with two children and yet my husband and I have never had intimate relations.

"Sometimes I wonder if this is sin *not* to have relations. I am a Christian and want to be in the center of God's will. I've prayed quite often about it and for some reason can't seem to get an answer. Perhaps this will be my answer from the Lord — your answer. Sometimes I long for sexual relations, and then again I think I'd abhor it. I am not sure how I *do* feel."

This represents an extreme condition in which both the husband and wife desperately need help. With much professional assistance one or both may change sufficiently to engage in normal relations, but it will undoubtedly require considerable time. As they come to understand the factors which have produced such extreme attitudes, the husband and wife will begin to think of sex in a very different, more normal light. There are other such cases on record of people who have responded unusually well to therapy. One advantage Arlene and her husband have is that they are both children of God. A Christian counselor can ultilize spiritual resources, thereby speeding the day when they may be sufficiently well-adjusted to be genuinely husband and wife.

The Unsatisfied Husband

Marriage at its best is marked by imperfection. Even "perfect couples" are quick to admit that not all runs smoothly. Husbands who become disillusioned when they start settling down in the realities of marriage find that many things may be wrong. High on the list of difficulties is sexual incompatibility. Although some women complain of their husbands' not meeting their needs, an even greater number of men confide that their wives do not satisfy them.

"I married one of the sexiest looking girls in the community," said one young husband, "but believe me, she turned out to be a cold potato." This, of course, is an old story. The Christian girl who is insecure and not naturally warm may try to reassure herself by adding to the outside what she doesn't feel inside. She may make every effort to dress the part, even though she doesn't feel the part. Sexual ability and responsiveness are not the result of a veneer. They emanate from a healthy body and mind, and a well-integrated personality. Likewise, sexual compatibility is the result of a happy marriage between two happy, well-adjusted people. A husband who is not satisfied sexually should look to himself to see if the problem lies with him. If not, it is usually a reflection of his wife's personality problems.

Dixie's problem

"My husband and I are Christians and have been married for ten years. The problem, as I see it, is one of sex. When I was a young girl, my father was in the habit of making sexual advances to me. I resented this because he was my father. He even suggested that I have relations with him so I wouldn't get into trouble because of curiosity with anyone else. He said that it was the father's duty to 'initiate' his daughter.

"My husband and I were finally able to have a normal sex life. However, it seems this past resentment of sexual advances rears its ugly head more now as I am older. Though I try not to show how I feel, sometimes my husband's advances are disgusting to me and I seem to be getting colder almost daily. I love him with all my heart and want to please him, and I have pretended warmth which he sometimes can see through. This naturally takes the happiness out of sex for him — and me. What can I do?"

Dixie was encouraged to talk her problem over with a Christian psychologist who found that it was much more severe than she had first indicated. Actually, they had never had really satisfying relations. After several counseling sessions Dixie began to discover and ventilate the causes for her problems. This brought some immediate relief. She came to realize that her husband was now about the age that her father was when he had made his advances to her as a child. By working through the problem, she was able to separate the two men — her husband and her father. Dixie's husband also went for several counseling sessions. Eventually the two achieved a much better adjustment.

Edith's problem

"My husband and I have been married for eight years and we have both gone to church every meeting since then.

"For some time he has been looking at other women. You see, my husband puts a lot of stress on sex. He feels that this is very essential. I do not really enjoy my sexual life. I go through the actions, but I have never felt the wonderful feeling that some girls do. Thus, he kept looking. At first I put up a fight, but later decided to ignore it.

"About two years ago he fell for an eighteen-year-old girl in our church. She began coming over for counseling and became a good friend. One thing led to another and one night I found them parked together, making love. He says he can't give up seeing her, because she meets his needs completely.

"After a short separation, we are back together. You see, my husband tells me that the other girl is passionate and really makes him feel like a man. He says she has a body and knows how to use it. I want him to change churches, but he will not. Some people have said that I am a failure as a wife or my husband never would have wandered. But this isn't so. I feel *he's* the one who needs help."

Problems like this are always tragedies, especially when they occur in the church and when they involve two so-called Christians. But an even greater tragedy is that nothing is done to help Edith and her husband. She feels she has been a dutiful and faithful wife. Consequently, if there is any changing to be done, it will have to be her husband who does it. She says, "It is really his fault," and, "He's the one who needs help." Then she states that she wants them to change churches. But changing churches is no solution. Since the problem is within Edith and her husband, they will take it with them wherever they go.

Her husband was certainly not right in committing adultery. But neither is Edith right in refusing to get her own life straightened out. Some women feel that because their husbands are Bible-believing Christians, there is no danger of their becoming unfaithful. Yet these same women will do nothing about getting professional help so that they can have normal sex relations. In other words, they hold the Scriptures over their husbands' heads and say, "I won't be a good wife to you and neither are you allowed to have relations with other women." Yet, these are the same women who comb the community, seeking sympathy if their husbands do find their satisfaction in another. Standing around quoting Scripture verses, or words of condemnation, will do little good. The solution is not in that direction. It is a humiliating experience for a woman to learn that her husband has turned to another woman for sexual satisfaction.

The self-righteous woman may explode and leave her husband, then in the name of the Bible make arrangements for a divorce. However, the more sensible and spiritual woman, while just as crushed, sits down and takes an inventory of herself by asking, "Why? What's wrong? Could it be I?"

Very often it is. When a man goes out with another woman, he usually does so because his needs are not met at home. Especially is this true of a man who professes to be a Christian. He has to be pretty desperate to override his standards and become involved with another woman. According to the Word of God, both husbands and wives are responsible to meet each other's needs. It is not one-sided.

Ben's problem

"I have a few questions regarding adjustments between a husband with strong sexual desires and a wife who is frigid:

1. Should they omit the physical side of married love?
2. Should the husband try to be satisfed with one-sided love?
3. Is the physical side of marital love necessary for a happy well-balanced marriage?
4. Will the husband be tempted with infidelity?
5. Will the husband lose the will to live and work?
6. Will frigidity have a separating effect between husband and wife?
7. What can a husband do to have a happy marriage with his frigid wife?

"My wife and I are both believers. When we were married, neither of us had experienced pre-marital relations. My wife is attractive and I suppose most men would even think she looks very appealing. But inwardly she is just the opposite — cold, nervous, and unresponsive. I love her very much and have done everything I know to help her, but nothing makes much difference.

"Frankly, I don't know how much longer I can go on this way. I pray that you can help us."

Ben's letter summarizes the feelings of many Christian husbands. They love their wives and want nothing to do with other women, but they are stymied because their mates refuse to get professional help. In the case of Ben, he did seek psychological counseling. Tests and interviews both revealed a well-adjusted Christian man. First attempts to persuade his wife to seek help failed. But after a year she reluctantly agreed. The psychologist found her to be a beautiful, well-poised young woman who made an excellent impression. But deep inside were strong, unbending attitudes which had developed since early childhood. After a few sessions she stopped therapy. After a few months, however, she started again. Finally she began to cooperate and get her feelings out in the open. She was amazed as she began to look at the unconscious material which had been buried for years. Little by little she became more cordial and relaxed, more genuinely honest with herself. Needless to say, this new attitude began to reflect itself in normal sex relations. Today she is still not free from problems, but she and her husband do have a much happier marriage. Divorce is not the Christian solution and neither is separation. God's solution is reconciliation and this often requires professional help.

Catherine's problem. Catherine is in her forties. For more than a year her husband, Allan, has noticed that she has become much more nervous and irritable than usual. In fact, they have had more arguments during the past year or so than they have had in their entire life combined. A time or two when she seemed to be especially unreasonable, he has accused her of being "off her rocker." This has only caused Catherine to "blow up" and create a bigger scene.

Catherine suspects that she is going through the menopause because her periods are non-predictable. However, she has not said much about it to Allan, and, in a way, she hates to admit it to herself. One night, after a bitter quarrel, Allan asked her if that was the problem. The two talked it over for awhile, then he insisted that she see the family physician. The next week, during her appointment, the doctor plainly told her, "Catherine, you are well into the menopause and these symptoms are all part of the picture." He recommended medication and talked to her about the emotional reactions of the menopause. She had already experienced most of them, so his words were no surprise to her. The doctor also talked to the husband and explained that he would have to be more patient for awhile. As time went by Catherine still had occasional upsets. But her husband understood why, and this kept him from developing feelings of resentment. Consequently, they were able to make a reasonably good adjustment during the "dangerous years" of married life.

Sexual Deviation

Through the years, I have been impressed with the large number of women who have written about their husband's sexual deviations. From every corner of the nation, indeed, from many parts of the world, letters have poured in regularly. These usually fall into two groups: (1) Those who tell of the extreme deviation of the husband and (2) those who ask if certain practices are normal. Some Christian wives know that their husbands are making demands which are far from those for which God has designed the human body. Other wives, however, are in a quandary. "Is this normal?" they ask. Then page after page they describe the gruesome orgies which please their husbands. The following complaint is typical:

"I am a Christian and I do not want to complain because I know that God has ordained sex in marriage. In fact, I have a great appreciation for this part of marriage. However, my husband demands such strange things that they seem very unnatural to me. When I hesitate to go along with him, he tells me that it is very normal and he gets angry if I don't submit. I have never talked to anyone about this — I am ashamed to, but I have reached the point where I can't put up with it any longer and I want to know if this is right in the sight of God.

"My husband and I met and were married at college. He graduated and now has two degrees. He has a long history of hurting people's feelings, being tactless and having a dictator's attitude.

"I frequently found, in my husband's possession, pictures of nude women which he used to excite himself. He even made me pose for photographs which he developed himself. These were taken when I was about three months pregnant and full breasted, which indicated to me that he was not satisfied with me the way I was ordinarily — small-breasted.

"On the whole, through my husband's seeming rejection of me as not being 'sexy' enough, and his domineering way, I have lost the love I had at first. However, I have tried to co-operate. What shall I do?"

You may think it strange that a husband (even a Christian) would ever get involved in such unnatural practices. However, a second look at the problem will reveal some causes. All human beings have problems, small or large. Even the best-adjusted people have to go through life carrying at least a moderate load of burdens. This is the result of our fallen natures. From the time our forefathers, Adam and Eve, sinned in the garden, we have been living under the curse. In short, we are an imperfect people living in an imperfect world under imperfect conditions. This means problems. Furthermore, we all show our problems in many different ways, and it is only natural that we try to compensate for those maladjustments through various means. In other words, if a woman, for example, has an inadequate, deprecating self-image, it is only natural for her to try to make up for this lack. If a hundred women had this same problem, they would probably employ at least a hundred different ways of trying to prove to themselves or to their friends that they actually did not feel inferior or insecure. Indeed, people find strange ways of compensating for their true feelings. Realizing this, it is understandable that some people show their maladjustment in sexual ways. Since sex is a strong, vital and even dramatic part of our human make-up, it is not surprising that many maladjustments find their expression in sexual ways.

A man, for example, may show his hostilities by shouting at his wife and children. Another man, on the other hand, may show his hostilities by refusing to talk. One husband may reveal his overwhelming insecurity by withdrawing from most social contacts, while another man may reveal his feelings of extreme insecurity by engaging in certain bizarre sexual practices or even by refraining from any normal relations. In fact, almost every kind of human maladjustment may very well reflect itself in sexual expressions.

Sexual practices have considerable significance. They are clues to more basic problems, or, on the other hand, to healthy personality adjustments.

Have you ever wondered why in private therapy a psychologist or psychiatrist eventually gets around to gaining information about a client's sex life? The answer, of course, is that a normal sex life tends to reflect a normal personality adjustment, whereas an abnormal sex life usually reflects serious personality maladjustments.

Sometimes a man who is a sexual deviate covers it quite completely. No one but his wife may know. To the people in the church or community he may appear to be a "perfect" husband. No one may suspect his deep disturbance. But when he comes to the psychologist's office and is given various psychological tests, these maladjustments begin to come to light. It is then the therapist is able to detect the problem.

Some men have developed extreme attitudes regarding sex because of their previous association with prostitute women or other lewd characters. Such men may have been accustomed to such relationships long before they were married. It is common knowledge that most women who offer their bodies for hire are cold and unresponsive, with little or no sexual feeling. In order to make up for this lack of real femininity and in order to attract customers, they engage in various types of deviation which even animals could never contemplate. A man who has been introduced to such practices and has continued in them may very well have developed responses which he comes to enjoy. In addition, his own lack of masculinity and his lack of ability to court and win a fine normal woman, causes him to continue in such deviate patterns. Many such men when coming into marriage are never happy until they cast their wife into a debased role and continue similar practices with her. Such was the case of the husband of the woman who wrote:

"My husband and I were married quite young, although he was four years ˌolder than I. My family was poor but it was respectable. My husband's family was also poor and, although I've only met his parents a few times (they're both dead now), I understand they didn't have any standards at all. In fact, my husband was on his own from about the time he was fourteen. Some time after we were married he told me that he started having affairs with prostitutes when he was only fifteen.

"He has often complained that I didn't give him the thrill that some of the other women did. So he wants me to do the same things they did with him.

"Dr. Narramore, you can't imagine the things he demands. Many times he has tied me down with a rope because he says it gives him an added thrill. Oh, I could go on and on, but it is so repulsive that I hate to even write it in a letter."

Sometimes a man feels that he is not getting the physical stimulus and thrill from sex which he would like to experience. Jokes and stories among male acquaintances may lead him to believe that unless he is utterly carried away into another world each time he has relations, he is not experiencing what other men have found. In addition, there are cheap magazines on sex which sometimes lead a man to believe that there is "much more than you had ever dreamed possible, if you only understood the techniques." So he begins to make unwholesome, disgusting demands on his wife, vainly searching for a little added thrill. Such men (and there are many) are looking to the goddess of sex for their life's fulfillment, rather than looking to Christ for their deep, abiding joy and happiness.

But these men can never find complete happiness through sex. God has created human beings in such a way that *they can only be happy in Him*. He has designed sex in such a way that it is important, and indeed satisfying. Yet, God has never intended that sex should fulfill more than a limited measure of our desire for happiness. Significant as it is, sex doesn't have that much to offer.

The solution to the longings of such men is faith in Christ who alone can fully satisfy the heart. Then, and only then, can sex take its rightful place and become most meaningful.

It is not unusual for a woman to complain that her husband mistreats her sexually and makes demands that are animalistic. To such a woman, sex is terrible and it is only to be tolerated, if not eliminated completely. Yet, a consideration of the facts often reveals something quite different. Such was the case of one woman who during her sessions with the marriage counselor told of her husband's "depravity." "Sex, sex, all he thinks of is sex," she kept saying. Further discussion revealed that the husband was normal in his desires, and that it was actually the wife who was abnormal in her disgust and hatred of anything sexual. True, her husband was a healthy, normal male who, like other Christian husbands, would have been happy to have had sexual relations frequently. But there was no trace of deviation. In such instances it is the *wife* who is deviate and who needs help.

How can a Christian wife help her husband who demonstrates bizarre sexual deviation?

The answers are several, but most important is that she understands that most sex problems are not organic in nature. Instead, they reflect a more basic personality disturbance. Armed with this insight, a woman can then look at her husband's problem, not so much with loathsome eyes as with eyes of compassion and understanding. She may be repulsed by his actions, but she can separate them from the man himself. She then is more apt to want to help him to become a well-adjusted Christian man. She realizes that he has not purposely taken this unnatural path — but that he has been deprived of certain basic emotional needs throughout childhood, adolescence and perhaps young adulthood. This has produced an adult whose sexual deviation is a signal that he is desperately in need of help "inside."

A wife can encourage her husband to talk about his early life and lead him into deeper understandings of his personality needs. Then when he sees that his sexual deviation is basically a personality problem, he will more likely respond to suggestions for professional help.

In summary, a problem of sexual deviation is never solved by continuing in it. It is not pleasant for the wife and, of course, it doesn't help her husband. It is not unusual that a Christian wife has to seek legal counsel in order to protect herself and also to encourage her husband to get help which he so badly needs. But she can usually help her husband most when she comes to a more thorough understanding of his problem, viewing it with kindness and Christian maturity. This, plus professional referral, have helped many men to become well-adjusted and to fill the responsible role into which God has called them.

CHAPTER TWELVE

Growing Spiritually

Life is a quest. But the greatest goal is as close as the opening of your heart. Sir Launfal searched the whole world for the Holy Grail and found it on his own doorstep when his heart was sundered by compassion.

But your search is not for a Holy Grail, a Golden Fleece or Camelot! It is a more desperate passion. How may it know fulfillment? In God alone, of course.

Does this sound shopworn and tiresome? Only because it is so seldom tried. As the poet has written:

"Baubles we buy with a soul's whole tasking
While only God may be had for the asking."

There is an unsuspected dividend in opening your heart and mind to God. The Lord Jesus said, "Seek ye first the kingdom of God, and His righteousness; and all these things shall be added unto you" (Matthew 6:33). God holds back no excellent thing from those who love Him with a full heart. The Saviour, as any discreet bridegroom, needs to know that you love him utterly — apart from the trinkets you think you need.

Probably no other name in history depicts the pinnacle of feminine fame more than that of the lovely Cleopatra. Here was a woman who had *everything*, if ever a woman did. Born a princess, of royal Grecian ancestry, she became the Queen of Egypt at twenty years of age. Her unusual beauty and feminine charm were matched only by her keen intellect and personal ambition. She was fabulously wealthy, living lavishly in the lap of luxury. She had power, prestige, and popularity. Her suitors were many and her lovers were men of power and renown. Her husband adored her and sacrificed his political achievements for the sake of her love. She was the mother of three promising children, heirs apparent to her kingdom. But at thirty-nine years of age she abruptly ended the chapter of her life by committing suicide.

Yes, Cleopatra had everything. Everything — except happiness. And happiness was something she longed for and strove for all her life — but never found.

The plot of her story has been rewritten in the lives of countless others down through the centuries. The world is shocked when a woman of beauty, fame and fortune gives way to her innermost despair and chooses to end it all rather than to go on living. Like Cleopatra, she has "everything to live for" — except happiness.

Every woman wants happiness, and she will seek it in many ways. From the time of Eve, women the world over have been seeking to regain the happiness that was lost by the deception of sin. A few have found it, and their hearts are filled with joy and satisfaction. But most seek without ever finding, because they have never come to the source of *true* happiness — Jesus Christ, the Son of God.

What are the things that women strive for in their pursuit of happiness? When they have achieved them, what then? Are they happy? Down through the annals of time, women have staked their hopes on all or part of the very elements possessed by Cleopatra; yet abiding happiness escaped them.

Love, security, riches and popularity — women strive to attain them in the never-ending search for happiness. They place a premium on beauty and charm, and spend great fortunes in trying to be glamorous. Talent is the envy of those who have none, while fame and fortune are the gods of those who do. The intelligent often look to education and science as the summit of satisfaction, while competent career girls climb to the crest of business ambition. Some seek serenity at the shrine of culture and the arts; others place power at the peak of perfection. Women the world over are looking for release from the tension and strain of an artificial society. They seek it in personal pleasure and moral abandon. Entertainment, thrills and excitement are the "pep pills" of disillusionment. The world pawns off counterfeits which unregenerate women treasure as gems.

Jesus said, "What shall it profit a man if he shall gain the whole world and lose his own soul?" (Mark 8:36). Indeed, at the end of the rainbow there is no pot of gold for the unbeliever; only disappointment, heartache and, in the end, a Christless eternity. For such, there is no *real* happiness on earth, and they have bypassed the road to Heaven.

The only source of genuine happiness comes from the Giver of Life and the Creator of all that is good. Truly, "Every good gift and every perfect gift is from above, and cometh down from the Father of lights, with whom is no variableness, neither shadow of turning" (James 1:17).

The most perfect gift ever given was the Son of God. This was the supreme sacrifice of love. "For God so loved the world, that He gave His only begotten Son, that whosoever believeth in Him should not perish, but have everlasting life" (John 3:16).

Have you accepted this most magnificent of all gifts — Jesus Christ, the Son of God? God offers Him to you as the only Way of salvation and eternal life. Will you be so foolish as to refuse Him?

You may think you do not need to make a personal decision for Christ. "I have always lived a good, respectable life, and I have tried to be kind and considerate of others. I'm sure that a good God will not condemn me for doing my best."

You are right. God does not condemn anyone for living a good life. But He *does* condemn all who reject His beloved Son. Christ said, "I am the Way, the Truth, and the Life: no man cometh unto the Father, but by Me" (John 14:6).

You may have gone to a lovely church all your life. You may have served the missionary society well. You may have spent much time and money for benevolent causes. This is commendable, but it is not enough. We are not saved by what *we* do, but rather by what *He* has already done on the cross of Calvary. "For by grace are ye saved through faith; and that not of yourselves: it is the gift of God: not of works, lest any man should boast" (Ephesians 2:8, 9).

It is right that you should do good and lead an honest, moral life. Those who don't, reap what they sow in misery and heartbreak. However, no matter how good you are, it is not good enough. No amount of human goodness, desirable though it may be, is good enough to meet God's standard of perfection. No honest person presumes to claim perfection. Christ is the only One who has ever lived a sinless life. He alone can fill God's standard of perfection. So, you see, the only access *anyone* ever has to God and to Heaven is through accepting Christ as the atonement for his sins. Everyone is saved in this same way. "Believe on the Lord Jesus Christ and thou shalt be saved, and thy house" (Acts 16:31).

When you accept Christ and commit your life to Him, you become the recipient of countless blessings. In the greatness of the Father's love for His child, He ". . . daily loadeth us with benefits . . ." (Psalm 68:19). Solomon, in immortal God-given wisdom, declared: "The blessing of the Lord, it maketh rich, and He addeth no sorrow with it" (Proverbs 10:22).

With perfection and abundance, Christ provides all that you have ever longed for or sought after. Love? There is no greater love than His love for you — a redeemed child of God. Security? You rest secure in His almighty hands. Riches? The wealth of all heaven is yours, and God will supply *all* your need according to His riches in glory. Christ is the essence of joy and peace. He satisfies the longing soul with His own goodness and turns their mourning into joy (Jeremiah 31:13). No one is happier than the child of God.

Through the centuries, millions of women have proved the power of God. The transformation in their lives, and in the lives of a multitude of women living today, bears testimony to the divine miracle of salvation. The following letters, from two different women, give evidence of His transforming power and love.

"Life was so meaningless. For years, instead of living, I just existed. It wasn't that I didn't have plenty that should have made me happy. My parents had money and I always had everything I wanted. Yet, I was miserable. Life seemed so shallow and empty and all the people I knew were so artificial. I didn't know there was One who loved me so much that He died for me — that there was One who could put meaning into my life.

"Then I received Christ. Now, instead of searching to find the meaning of life, I know the One who has given me eternal life. I can truly say that Jesus satisfies.

"I am happier now than I have ever been in my life. This thing is too good not to share. I want to tell all I can about Jesus and His wonderful love."

A second lady wrote:

"I corresponded with you some time ago and told you about my troubles. I was so discouraged that I didn't know where to turn. However, a lot has happened in the meantime. Early this month, during a special service in our church, the Holy Spirit convicted me of sin, and for the first time, I saw myself as I really was — a miserable sinner in desperate need of a Saviour. The knowledge that Jesus died on the cross and shed His innocent blood for my sins completely overwhelmed me. I went forward, letting the tears fall as I came. The pastor and others counseled with me. I know now I am saved, not by the way I feel, but because God's wonderful Word says so. I know I am a 'new creature' — something I could not understand before.

"God has worked wonders in my life. I am no longer haunted by my troubles. Since my conversion, the unhappy past has been erased from my mind. I feel free, and I sleep very well now, whereas in the past I would often be troubled by terrible dreams and nightmares. But that's all in the past, and now I have a peace and a calm which exceeds anything I have ever experienced before. I can truly say, 'The joy of the Lord is my strength' (Nehemiah 8:10), for He has proved it in my life."

Trophies of grace! Like countless others, these two women are living demonstrations of the miraculous change that takes place in a life when Christ comes in to dwell.

Not long ago, I talked with two Christian ladies whom I had known through the years. What interested me was this: one had stopped growing spiritually shortly after she was saved, but the other was continually making advances for Christ, and had become an unusual blessing to many.

One was standing still. Her life once held radiant promise but was now shallow and ordinary. There is no reproach on the blossoms of Maytime if they yield their course to October fruit. Both are perfect in their season. But the blossom that refuses to form fruit of any kind may provoke the heart of God as did the fruitless fig tree in the encounter with Christ.

But how can the Christian woman guard against a spiritually-dwarfed existence? How may an office girl, a homemaker, or a professional woman reach the spiritual stature to which she is ordained?

Exercising Your Will. The first step toward spiritual development is always the same: *surrender.* This means *wanting to change.* Unless you exercise *your* will, you will never have *God's* will. It all started in the Garden of Eden. God gave the human race intelligence and the power to choose or reject, and He has never revoked that privilege. The poet Ella Wheeler Wilcox expresses the importance of the will in these lines:

> "One ship drives east and another drives west
> With the self-same winds that blow.
> 'Tis the set of the sails and not the gales
> That tell us the way to go."

The stuff of life is much the same for everyone. *The difference is what you want to do.* If you are to become the woman you are capable of becoming, you must say to God, "I want to grow. I want to be controlled by the Holy Spirit. Today and each day hereafter I will surrender to You. Teach me and guide me."

This is what will begin to distinguish you from ordinary women. This act of your will does not assure you of easy sailing. But it does guarantee that you will be moving in the right direction and that inch by inch you will approach a spiritual maturity that can only end in blessing. The spiritual pilgrim can hardly expect to progress if he is not yielded to the one who is loved and emulated — in this case the risen Saviour and Lord who today is at God's right hand. Accompanying this act of the will comes an absorption and trust that will mount on the promises of God, even as a vine lifts its tendrils to the sun, and at the same time is enabled to put down thirsty roots into good water and soil.

Meditating on God's Word. No less important than your attitude is a second axiom of spiritual growth — *drinking daily at the fountain of God's Word.* This should have no strange sound to the Christian. Natural life fades away in the absence of food. Can spiritual life thrive without nourishment?

As natural food contains a maze of marvelous components — proteins, fats, carbohydrates, complex vitamins, enzymes and many as yet undiscovered monitors of good health, so does God's Word serve as a perfect nutriment for growth as well as a corrective purge for that which inhibits health and growth. After all, the Saviour, who is the incarnate Word, bears the name of the Bread of Life, and the Judean village of Bethlehem bore in its Hebrew meaning the prophetic term, "House of Bread." The Bread of Life was bruised and broken on Calvary in order to become the source of life and health for a lost world.

A special time and place is good practice for Bible reading. But thirsty Christians have found a variety of times and places for the refreshment of their spiritual lives, no matter the hour or surroundings.

Frequently, published meditations for daily Bible reading have been made available in single page devotions. Many of the richest illustrations and applications of God's Word through Christian history have been thus presented. Yet, you will likely find that the enjoyment of the Bible — God's love letter to you — will need to be a personal matter, far beyond delectable samplers, pre-digested concentrates or pharmaceutical supplements.

Prayer. If anything follows closely the reading of God's Word it is *communion,* usually referred to as prayer. The very word "union-with" speaks of a togetherness of the heart with God.

You can never do wrong in saying any number of times a day, "Lord Jesus, I love You." This is far from a mere automatic employment, as the sadly empty, "O Jewel in the Lotus," of the Buddhists. It will take fire from heaven. And you cannot love someone with all your heart without wanting to please this One.

Communion involves listening to God even as prayer mainly suggests speaking with God. Both are the means by which you may "mount up with wings as eagles."

Unbalanced books can be the bane of a business office. Prayer offers an opportunity to enter all known human factors into the ledgers of God so that our omniscient Saviour may have our bared hearts upon which to display His grace and glory in providing and overruling our infinite lack. Robert Morrison, who translated the Bible into Chinese, said, "Keep short accounts with God." He certainly had to, as his native assistants labored in such momentary fear of death from Chinese authorities that they carried poison daily upon their persons. We need communion in prayer whether we are in peril or peace.

Fellowship. Fellowship is another principle of spiritual growth, and a corollary of communion. If we love God, *we truly must love each other,* the latter being the very proof of the former.

This has more to it than first appears. For one thing, we are always becoming like those with whom we associate. Subconsciously we even come to resemble them in posture, speech, and manner. This is well-known concerning lovers, young and old. It is often seen in young ministers who have so ardently admired the saintly old warriors of the faith. And it recalls the fable of Baucis and Philemon, the ancient Greek couple who came to look like each other unto immortality. If we want to grow into mature Christians we should fellowship with others who love and serve the Lord.

Worship. Another growth factor concerns *church attendance* on the Lord's Day. This has nothing primarily to do with the style of the meeting place. Actually the New Testament church seems to have flourished in private homes without having encountered problems of real estate and the concerns of a complex organization. The church was seen as the emerging "body" and "bride" of the Saviour, an organism with only incidental organizational lines.

Meeting with God's people is certainly not open to option. It is a wholesome requirement. God tells us not to forsake the assembling of ourselves together. What can be more satisfactory than this warm tempering of personalities, which remain at the same time forever individual in the traits God gave them? You may think of the blood-redeemed Christian assembly as the poet's "dome of many-colored glass, staining the white radiance of eternity." Andrew Mitchell said of this: "Mutuality and individuality find their most beautiful blending in Christianity."

Literature. The rising flood of excellent Christian literature offers a further channel of spiritual growth. As you walk into Christian bookstores, your eyes fall upon almost numberless books and pamphlets.

No language, ancient or modern, has ever served so many millions of homes as the English tongue. For this, the American woman may well be the envy of the Christian world. With this privilege, however, comes a grave responsibility. While there is an abundance of Christian literature that can change a woman, many women never take the time to read it. Such was the case of Ellen. She hadn't read a Christian book in years, if then! True, she was busy, like most other women, but she didn't understand the value of books, nor did she sense the true proportions of her need.

In contrast, Deborah also lived within the confines of a busy schedule. But she knew that she could not afford to live on an ordinary plane, and that reading would help her to live well. Children, diapers, dishes, meals, and a hundred other things filled her days and nights. But from time to time she picked up a Christian book and read a few pages.

In a year she was surprised to realize that she had actually read several volumes.

What had this done for Deborah? It had taken her out of her "confinement" and had given her associates whom she could never have met in her local community. She had pushed back her horizons and had gained a picture of how God was dealing with His children throughout the world.

Music. Another incalculable influence in your spiritual growth is music. Through the centuries it has been the very handmaid of the gospel message. In our own day, many gifted musicians have presented the Gospel in song to a host of homes through technically excellent recordings, even to the fine nuances of high fidelity and stereo rendition.

No less inspiring are the composing careers of present-day Christian musicians whose tapestry of lyrics comes from Scripture portions wedded to melodies of heavenly tenderness. Quartets, organ selections and instrumental programs are multiplying today across the airwaves of Christian radio stations. You need not be as Opal who confessed that she had never heard of Christian radio. She revealed that she had been wasting much of her time listening to the muddy patter of a noisy disc jockey, coupled with the hypnotic jingles about cigarettes, beer, and wine. The whole tone of her experience began to improve with the change of a wholesome and inspirational music diet. Opal rose, from a commonplace and nervous condition of dial-twisting, to a serene Christian mother who was influenced by Christian music to establish a new order in her home.

Witnessing. Witnessing for Christ offers a crowning experience in your Christian growth. The definition of a witness is quite simple: a person who knows something from personal observation or experience and who merely states the truth and circumstances of this fact. Similarly, a Christian witness speaks of a personal salvation experience, based upon the person and atoning work of Jesus Christ. This does not mean arguing or instructing. It merely involves your telling what has happened to you. This cannot be debated.

The religious leaders of Israel, for example, could not dislodge the simple man whose back-to-the-wall statement rang out deathless across the whole church age: "Whereas once I was blind, now I see."

Actually, your influence as a Christian woman is very important. As you witness for the Lord you are doing these things: You are helping others to learn about the only One who can save them from their sins, and you are being obedient to God. A mandate for all witnessing is found in Romans 1:16: "For I am not ashamed of the gospel of Christ: for it is the power of God unto salvation to everyone that believeth; to the Jew first, and also to the Greek."

How can you be a witness in your own home or office? This is not the problem it first seems to be, when you think of the lives you touch each day.

Perhaps you would like to give an attractive tract to a fellow-worker or to those who call at your door. Some Christians have found that Christian books and magazines are among the best ways to influence others for Christ. But regardless of your methods, witnessing is not something to be labored. It is the natural overflowing of love for Christ.

A woman's world! One filled with spiritual possibilities. As a woman, you were born to believe and to believe in God. You were born to believe in God through His Son, the Lord Jesus Christ. You were born to minister across the ages. You have produced the kings, the emperors, the generals, the teachers, the artists, and the common toilers of this world.

Do you dare to live without God?

As a woman, you may achieve many things. With keenness of mind, intuitive perception and remarkable gifts, you may ascend to great heights. But nothing you might attain can ever equal the greatness of, or befit your queenliness more than growing in the very image of Christ. *This is your greatest achievement!*